Also by Genevieve Davis

Secret Life, Secret Death
the Book and the DVD

The true story of a young mother, who fell into bootlegging and prostitution in Gangland Chicago in the Roaring 20's. And her granddaughter, who hunts down the family secret.

Available at www.october7thstudio.com

Coming later in 2014:
The Brides' Tale: An erotic tale of star-crossed lovers in medieval Italy

Fanni's Viennese Kitchen

Austrian Recipes and Immigrant Stories

Fanni in 1908 in Vienna

Fanni's Viennese Kitchen

Austrian Recipes and Immigrant Stories

Genevieve Davis

October 7th Studio

Genevieve Davis

www.october7thstudio.com

This is a work of non-fiction

Milwaukee, WI

Printed in U.S.A.

Cover and Book Design by Genevieve Davis

Front & Back Cover Pictures – Collection of the Author

First Edition

Dedication

To Fanni, Johann, Margaret and Helen

Contents

Chapter 4

Veggie Dishes

69

Fresh Bean Salad, Potato Salad, Cucumber Salad, Red Cabbage, Vegetables with Toasted Crumbs, Einbrenn, Kohlrabi, Boiled Potatoes, Pan Roasted Potatoes, Pickles, Iceberg Salad, Green Salad, Horseradish Sauce

Chapter 5

Johann and the Summerhouse

87

Chapter 6

Jelly, Beverages, Wine

99

Grape Juice, Root Beer, Coffee, Grape Wine, Lemonade

Chapter 7

Life In Vienna

111

Genevieve Davis

Acknowledgments

Thanks to Mom and Aunt Margie and her daughter Betty for their work codifying these recipes! Thanks to Renate for her recipes.

Thanks to Mom for reading this manuscript, making comments and corrections and translating letters. Thanks also for travel diary notes and sharing lots of stories about Fanni.

Thanks to my friend Lynn Weiborg for proofing and to David Glaeser for reading the stories, and for help with German translations and military history.

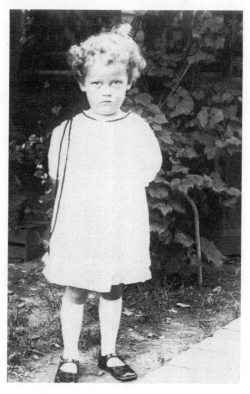

My Mom was hiding behind the summerhouse because she didn't want her Dad to take this picture

Fanni and I wading at Devil's Lake

Introduction

I hope to pass along to you my Grandmother Fanni Baier's recipes, in a way that you can also get to know who she was, and how she approached life. Fanni's cooking was an integral part of a whole experience with a lady, who not only made an art out of preparing authentic Austrian dishes, but also shared her simple - but never simplistic - outlook on life. She did that by example, lighting the way for me and many other people.

This book forms a portrait of Fanni, comprised not only of recipes, but also stories about her fortunes in life, my experiences as a child finding refuge at Fanni's house from the turbulence in my own home, and funny stories about Fanni intervening on my Mother's behalf, when my Mom was a young woman. There are also many photos of Fanni, from her days in Vienna as a young woman to her time as an elderly lady living in the lower flat of her own duplex in Milwaukee. That's where she was living by the time I knew her.

"Fanni" is pronounced the Austrian way – "Fah-nee." Fanni was short for Franziska, a name my Grandmother apparently didn't like. In America, she always used the anglicized "Frances" when she wrote out her first name.

Fanni usually cooked by feel. So most of these recipes I have collected from my Mom or her sister, Margaret, or Margaret's daughter Betty. They are Fanni's authentic recipes, which my Mom, aunt, and cousin codified with ingredient amounts and cooking directions. A few recipes come from Rosa, Mom's friend in Austria. Several come from Fanni's niece Fini (also called Rudi), Fini's daughter Renate and

Renate's son Bernhard. A few recipes Fanni actually copied out in her own hand – one for Grape Juice, several Pickle recipes, Marble Cake, Red Devil's Food Cake and one for *Murbeteig*, a kind of Austrian shortcake which you pile with fruit, and bake.

Some recipes are "cook by feel recipes," that I reconstructed, or that Mom took down with just the ingredients. So if you don't like to cook by feel, just stick to the codified, kitchen tested recipes! All the recipes are fun to read, in any event.

If you are into gluten-free cooking, you can substitute almond meal for bread crumbs. You can also use potato or tapioca flour for thickening stews and gravies. You can substitute rice flour, as I did for my version of crepes in Mehlspeise, which makes for an even tastier dish. I like health food, so I have included a few of my variations on what Fanni cooked. I still enjoy making variations on her dishes. I also get to enjoy eating them when my Mom or Betty makes them.

What impressed me the most about my Grandmother, Fanni, wasn't her Austrian cooking, which was amazing in and of itself. It was her outlook that was even more amazing to me, considering the many hardships she had to confront over a lifetime. Fanni was always cheerful. And she always thought the best of people. She didn't judge people by their actions, but rather loved them for who they were. As my Mother likes to say, "She had one personality for all occasions."

Now I have a lot of Fanni's furniture and household things, which I enjoy using, because they remind me of her. Many years after I had long lost all the mittens that Fanni had made for me, my Mother gave me a Christmas present – a pair of gray, handmade mittens from Grandma, that had once belonged to my Aunt Margie. Wow! Now, over two decades after Fanni was gone, I had another pair! At first I just wore them when I went out for a walk in the cold weather, to save them. But now I wear them everyday in the winter and have mended them many times over. I wish I could give them to Fanni to mend, because then you wouldn't be able to tell they'd been mended at all.

Fanni had also given me her two sets of earrings. Initially she had advised my mother not to let me get my ears pierced, because she said it would make my ear lobes longer and the holes would stretch out. But after a few years, Mom relented and let me have a doctor pierce them, at my own expense, when I was in high school. Then, Fanni gave me two pairs of earrings, a gold pair and a silver pair, neither of which she wore any more, because her ears had closed up.

Those earrings are so special to me. But to my nearly eternal disappointment, I lost one of the gold earrings. I kept its mate for years hoping the other one would turn up. Waiting, hoping, waiting. In the meantime, I moved several times, and each time the other earring didn't show up when I reorganized everything. But I kept hoping. Then one year on my birthday, I was rummaging around my jewelry box that Grandpa had made, and found BOTH earrings. *That* was a really great birthday present!

Sunday Dinner at Fanni's on 20th Street

Left to Right: Mom, Fanni, Johnny, Betty, Herman, Johann, Robby [my older brother.] I think Margaret is behind Mom. Dad's not in it because he usually took the pictures. I'm not in it, either, because I was born a couple of years later.

Chapter 1

Cooking at Fanni's
Fanni's Kitchen
Shopping Rounds
Sunday Dinner

Cooking at Fanni's

Fanni's cooking was an amazing form of alchemy, in which she transformed the most humble of ingredients into delicious dishes. As she worked, she clomped in her cuban heels back and forth from the kitchen table to the stove to the hanging pantry, over the back stairs, to the icebox a few steps down on the landing to the basement. Gradually, a wonderful cloud of aromas traveled out into the dining room, the hub from which all the other rooms radiate. So no matter where you are in the house, sooner or later the comforting smells of the next meal beckon you with their fragrance. Sometimes hours went by while I played in the living room with Fanni's games and toys, hearing the sounds, two rooms away, of Fanni stirring, chopping, pounding, and clinking, punctuated by the creaking of the oven door spring. The aromas grew stronger and stronger, until finally Fanni announced, "Komm essen!"

Fanni often sang songs in German as she made good things to eat. She seldom used recipes when she cooked, using "a little of this and a little of that. It has to feel right," she used to say.

Therefore, the recipes in this book all came from her. Her daughters codified the ingredients. There are some recipes I reconstructed, either from talking to Mom, or from thinking about it. I even have a few recipes in Fanni's handwriting. I think she copied those out of the newspaper, the Gridley Dairy cookbook, took them down from a friend or wrote them out for someone. In any event, all the recipes are authentically Fanni's, with a few extras thrown in, experiments from my kitchen and Mom's.

Fanni's Kitchen

Fanni used lard in her cooking, which gives extra flavor, but you'll probably want to substitute with butter or olive oil for today's healthy eating. Occasionally, she did use butter in her cooking. She also kept a can of congealed bacon fat, which she had collected from frying bacon in a skillet. That was to "schmier" on rye bread as a snack. Cholesterol hadn't been "invented" yet in Fanni's lifetime, so no one was worried about that, though perhaps they should have been.

Fanni had an assortment of enameled pots and pans. And she used different sized cast iron frying pans in her cooking. They had a nice, heavy bottom and cleaned up easily, because they were seasoned. If your cast iron cookware doesn't clean up well, try heating your pan good and hot. Then melt some beeswax in it and rub it all over the inside with a cloth. While still hot, wipe the excess off. That's something I saw a mountain man do at a re-enactment and it works really well! You can also use your favorite kind of cooking oil to season an iron skillet.

Fanni's choice of spices were salt and black pepper, paprika (either hot or mild), bay leaf, cloves, caraway seeds, nutmeg, dried marjoram and thyme and fresh parsley, which she kept in a glass of water on the sink or the kitchen table. She also used chives from the yard.

Bread crumbs were a staple in Fanni's kitchen and she used them in many of her dishes. She didn't buy them, but made them herself, from dry, stale Kaiser rolls, which the bakery would throw in with her regular order, at no charge. She grated the stale rolls and then pounded them into crumbs.

These she browned in butter and poured over vegetables like brussels sprouts, cauliflower or asparagus. They added a nice flavor and crunch. If you're doing gluten-free cooking, you can get the same effect with almond flour. She also used stale Kaiser rolls for her wonderful bread dumplings, shaving them with a paring knife into *schnibbles* (small pieces).

Schnibbles is a nice word. My Mom used it to refer to the bits of paper I would strew around an art project. I would leave them where they lay when I finished one project and moved on to the next creation. Mom would scold, "Pick up all these *schnibbles!*" interrupting my creative train of thought with her Austrian idea of order and neatness. This struggle eventually evolved into a gridlock, when I was a teenager, over cleaning up my room, which would not only be strewn with art and craft junk, but just about everything that had once lived in my two dressers. If Mom had only understood that this was a sign that she had a creative child, perhaps she would have found the whirlwind condition of my bedroom a little more fascinating. In fact, when I was a little kid, Mom recalls she was sleeping in my room one night and woke up in the dark to see me busy playing away with my toys and "jabbering." She watched me from her cot, fascinated, as I played away and jabbered on for hours, apparently oblivious that my Mom was watching me.

At Fanni's, beef bone soup was a daily, nourishing start for the evening meal, something Johann insisted on, too. Every few days Fanni started a big pot of water boiling, tossed in a soup bone and a chopped up an onion, and let that simmer on the back of the stove, to blend the flavors. She added other stuff toward the end, like barley, carrots and celery, and a potato if she had one. If she lucked out on her shopping rounds, she got the ham bone from the butcher's.

She scraped all the meat and fat off the bone, scooped out the marrow and put it all in the soup.   During the Depression years, this was often the only thing she had to serve for dinner.   But it was nutritious.   Of course, the smell permeated the house, which her little daughter, my Mom, didn't find appetizing.   Mom grew up hating to eat soup, not to mention daily servings of farina and oatmeal at breakfast!

Fanni didn't do a lot of baking in her tiny kitchen, preferring instead to stop in at the bakery twice a day for fresh long johns, crullers and jelly rolls, along with fresh bread and hard rolls.   Friends and neighbors often dropped in for an impromptu "Kaffee Klatsch," so she always kept a coffee pot on the back of the stove and had sweet rolls or cake in the house to serve.   On hot summer days, she had a nice custom of making a big pitcher of fresh lemonade from lemons she squeezed herself.   She floated slices of the fruit on it and served that on the front porch, where the ladies could sit in the open air on a wicker chair or the porch swing and catch a breeze, while they watched the traffic stop and start at the stop light on the corner of 20th and Highland, in Milwaukee.

Fanni baked items she couldn't get at the bakery.   She made plum, apricot or apple kuchen, depending on what fruits were in season at the time.   For the Christmas holidays, she always made her fabulous apple strudel, an all day affair. The dough had to be carefully rolled out, stretched and pulled without it breaking.   This was done on a special board, about 4 feet by 4 feet square.   She had the dough pulled out so it was paper-thin and you could read a newspaper through it. Then she filled the strudel and rolled it up, very carefully to avoid tears, cut the roll in half and formed two horseshoe-shaped loaves for baking.   It was quite an amazing feat!   For tips on how she did that, see Apfelstrudel in Desserts.   You can also cheat and use ready-made phyllo dough!

Shopping Rounds

Before she had a fridge, Fanni put her shopping bag over her arm and made the rounds of the stores first thing in the morning, to get supplies she needed for that day.   That's the European style of the marketing.   She visited the butcher shop, the bakery, and the Ma and Pa grocers on the corner. The proprietors stood behind the counter and greeted her by name.   She would tell them what she needed and they would fetch and bag her items for her.   Often she went to the drug and hardware stores on her daily rounds, too.   The shops were all within a four block radius of her home on 20th and Highland, but the whole circuit took a couple of hours, because no matter what her route, she would run into friends along the way, and stop and chat with them.   I remember shrinking to hide behind the skirt of Grandma's dress when we ran into her friends, who were naturally friendly and curious about me.   Sometimes I went with her when she stopped up at the dark green, wooden stalls of the farmer's market on 17th and Fond du Lac.   I also remember walking with my mitten over my nose, because of the stink of hops in the air, that descended in foul smelling clouds from the breweries: the Schlitz Brewery on 3rd, the Pabst on 10thand Miller west of downtown.

When Fanni's daughter Helen, my Mom was a little girl, she loved to go with her mother on her rounds, because the shopkeepers gave her treats.   She got a cold wiener at the butchers, a cruller at the bakery, an apple or some penny candy on display at the grocer's counter, like pink and white sugar coated licorice snaps.   It was an impressive haul for a little kid.   I still find little pink and white licorice snaps under the couch cushions at Mom's, when I take them off and put them on the floor to make a bed at her house.   The butcher that Fanni always did business with, Butcher Kahn, the one who always handed Mom a cold wiener as a treat – apparently, according to Mom, he hacked up his wife.   That was the only crime Mom ever heard of when she was a child.

One time Fanni and little Helen were shopping for clothes up on 12th and Vliet Street.   Fanni pronounced the name of the street the Viennese way, "Fleet Street." Up there were dress shops, shoe stores, cleaners and the big department store, Schusters. That's where my five-year old Mom decided one day, to disappear.   When Fanni noticed my Mom was missing and couldn't find her, she talked to the police.   They looked for her, but Mom wasn't in the store, and the police finally had to tell a frantic Fanni to go home to wait for news.   Then when Fanni got home, there was my five-year old Mom, waiting for her on the steps.   Somehow Mom had gotten it in her head to walk home by herself.

Vliet Street was also where they gave away dishes at the Colonial Theater during the Depression, to get people to come out and spend a little change at the movies.   On Dish Night, everyone who came got a free dish.   That's where Fanni, Helen and her sister Margaret got the poppy dishes Fanni used for everyday.

You'd think that people like Fanni and Johann, who had grown up on farms in Austria, would grow their own vegetables.   But for some reason, they never did that, even when everybody had a "victory garden" during World War II to supplement their rations.   During the summer growing season, Fanni got fresh fruits and vegetables from a farmer, who came by several times a week and parked his big open truck with a canopy on her block.   Fresh veggies were a rarity at that time in grocery stores.   All the ladies who lived on Fanni's block congregated around the truck, so they could pick out what they wanted, haggle a good price and enjoy a Klatch together [a little gossip].   That's how Fanni met other ladies and made friends.   She met Mrs. Habenicht that way, the mother of ten children, the same the lady whose husband commissioned Johann to build them a house in Germantown, at a time when Johann badly needed the work.

Sunday Dinner

Sunday at Fanni's was the day to savor the parade of flavors on the table.   It was the day when Fanni pulled out all the stops for our big family dinner.   "She could never attend church, because she was cooking all morning," Mom says. Unlike Fanni, we had to go to Mass, so by the time we drove in the car down to the inner city to Grandma's, it was about noon.   The dining room table we ate on was a handsome piece of furniture, with lathe turned legs and inlaid wood that her husband Johann had built - with salvaged wood, the way he always made everything.   A tablecloth protected it and the dishes were laid by me, when I was old enough, along with my mom, her older sister, Margaret or her daughter Betty. Grandpa also built the china cabinet, with glass windows on the doors, where we got out the fancy yellow dishes, with pink and blue flowers on the rim.   Her silver plate was kept in a blue felt-line box in a drawer.   Someone tall, like my Dad or my Uncle screwed in the light bulbs in the chandelier.

Someone else pushed in the mother-of-pearl button on the wall for the light switch, and the yellow plates and polished silverware gleamed brilliantly under half a dozen bulbs perched above.

In from the kitchen in the hands of my mother or aunt came the soup, something like liver dumpling soup. Then baked chicken arrived, with gravy or Wiener Schnitzel, or briny, vinegary Lammfleish with rice [Sauerbraten made with lamb]. This was accompanied by side dishes like brussels sprouts with their slightly bitter taste or cauliflower, always drizzled with browned, buttered bread crumbs. And for every big dinner, Fanni made bread dumplings, the size of door knobs, with the delicious taste of fresh bread. After being hailed several times, finally Fanni emerged from the kitchen, sat down and joined us, the apples of her cheeks flushed from cooking all morning. Then we oohed and ahhhed our appreciation for the feast she gave us.

Finally, after second and third helpings, the women collected the plates and took them into the kitchen, where Fanni would be getting things ready for dessert. She had me beat heavy cream with a crank-operated eggbeater. I did that until my arms were too sore to continue and then she took over. That whipped cream went on the jello and in coffee. A white bakery box was placed on the table. Someone pulled the string that had been tied in a bow, pushed up the lid and took out a glazed orange cake, or an angel food cake. But the best was for birthdays, when a large white box sat on the table, its cellophane window giving a glimpse of a fancy birthday cake. It had garlands of squiggled butter frosting and soft pink roses with green leaves artfully squeezed out of a pastry bag, which surrounded a personalized birthday greeting, written in colored frosting.   They always cut a piece with a rose for me.

Finally, it was time for the big cleanup.   Mom remembers how they sang together every night while they washed dishes in her childhood.   I don't remember hearing that on Sundays.   Just the groaning and snoring of the men who had retired into the living room to loaf and digest, while I played with Grandma's toys.

Before that, when I was a toddler, they'd put me down to sleep after dinner in Uncle Herman's room.   Sleep came quickly.   But I remember plenty of times waking up with night terrors and bolting through the lace curtain in the doorway, into the blinding light of the dining room to seek comfort from my Dad or Mom, who by that time were eating again, with the rest of the family.   They were munching a sandwich dinner of cold cuts, like *liebercase* and *braunschweiger mit die speck* [liverwurst with bacon bits] that Johnny, Margaret's husband, made at Connie Fischer's Handgemachte Wurst.   Some of the grownups spread raw hamburger on their rye bread, along with horseradish.   They all drank coffee.

Finally, when all the eating was over, one of the men stood up with a handkerchief in hand and loosened the bulbs in their sockets, because they were too hot to touch with fingers.   We sat around some more until all the dishes were done. Then it was time to drive home in the dark and return to our lives, without the calm and order of Fanni's'.

Mom

Fanni with Johann

Chapter 2

Soups

When we were staying with Grandma for a day or two, she'd make soup, like liver dumpling soup. Her mastery came from many years of making soup for Johann, who always wanted it as an appetizer at the beginning of the meal.

"It was always the same soup," groans my mother, who consumed it day in and day out during her childhood. Mom explains what was in the soup in the Depression years, when that might just be the whole meal. "She used a beef bone, carrots, celery and potatoes. Sometimes it had rice in it, which Uncle Herman, our roomer, would get when he took the red coaster wagon over the viaduct, to where they were dispensing commodities. He'd come home with lots of rice and barley and flour."

Fanni and Johann didn't qualify for government food, because they owned their house. "When Grandpa had a job again, and there was money, Fanni would boil a whole chicken to make stock for the soup."

When I went to Fanni's and she prepared a big pot of soup, she kept me occupied with the papery onion skins, feathery carrot tops and grungy potato peels. We put these into an enamel saucepan with a little water. Then her soup went on the gas stove with the tall legs. Mine went on, too, but without a flame underneath it. We stirred my soup with the old worn silver plate tablespoon she used as a cooking spoon, and pretended to slurp a taste of my soup out of the pan. "Ya, dat tastes so gut!" she marveled.

That was the only time I ever saw Fanni enter the realm of make-believe, which was pretty much my favorite place to be when I wasn't staying over at her house.

Tomato Soup

Codified by Mom

6 medium tomatoes

1 pint water

4 cloves

½ onion, chopped

2 tsp. sugar

1 tsp. salt

dash of cinnamon

1/8 tsp. baking soda

2T butter

2T flour

Cook tomatoes with water, cloves, onion, sugar, salt and cinnamon for 20 minutes.   Strain.

Reheat and add soda (this cuts the acidity).

Melt butter, add flour with a wire whisk or make a paste, and pour hot strained tomato mixture gradually into flour/butter mixture.

Beef Soup

Beef bone

Celery with leaves

Onion

Carrots

Potato or barley or rice

Salt and pepper

Boil the above ingredients, except the starches, for an hour or more.   Clean the bone and then throw the meat in the pot. Add some barley or some potatoes or some rice and cook until done.

Chicken Soup

Chop up and boil back, neck, liver, gizzards, heart for one hour in a 2 quart sauce pan.   Add potato and carrots.   Boil 20 minutes.   Add a little fresh parsley a few minutes before serving.

If you're feeling flush, boil the whole chicken for soup.   If you want the real taste of chicken, get one from a farm that raises them the way Fanni got them – organic, no hormones, no antibiotics, free range critters that run around outside and peck at worms and greens.   Factory chickens are evil.

Chicken Soup Dumplings

Farm Eggs

Flour

Salt

Water

Potatoes, put through a ricer [optional]

Mix the above ingredients together to make a stiff paste. Drop by teaspoonfuls into simmering soup and boil a few minutes.

My Variation with Herbs from the Garden

Add fresh chopped herbs from the garden to the dumpling batter, such as basil, oregano, thyme.

My Variation, with a Lot of Flavor!

Boil a leg or breast, along with several cloves of garlic, onion, and optional ginger root, salt and cayenne pepper for one half hour.   Add sliced carrots and potatoes and optional mushrooms and boil for another 20 minutes until veggies are done.   Right before serving, add chopped parsley.   If you opted for the ginger root, squeeze a fresh lemon into the soup. If you did not opt for ginger, add some fresh chopped basil along with the parsley.

Nockerln

Reconstructed with Mom

Eggs

Flour

Milk

Salt

Mix the above together to make a thick paste. Drop by teaspoons full into the soup.

Nockerln are a traditional feast item in Austria for St. Leopold's Day, often served with Goulash, (included here in Meat Dishes). Celebrated on November 15, St. Leopold's Day is also a day to sample the new wine, cook a goose or stuff a featherbed with goose feathers.

Leopold was a royal prince and margrave of Klosterneuberg. He turned down the imperial crown, when it was offered to him upon his brother's death. Canonized in 1486, he fathered 18 children, which perhaps is why he is the patron saint of large families and the protector of dead children. He also founded the Klosterneuburg Abbey.

My cousin, Ingrid, Fanni's great niece, now has a second home in Klosterneuberg, the same town where he once lived. There she grows a profusion of potted plants on the patio and likes to curl up with her cat, Suzy Peter, next to a cozy ceramic stove she had built into her house.

Excerpt, Mom's Vienna Travel Diary

Sunday, July 19. Pouring rain and cold. Went to church at Arsenal, then to Fini's, [Fanni's niece] where we were invited for Sunday dinner. She is a marvelous cook and must have spent days preparing authentic Viennese specialties. We found her very pleasant and kind-hearted. She's an old-fashioned, motherly lady who loves to see people eat her cooking.

The first course at her house was Griesnockerln soup, (small dumpling soup), made from scratch, with her own stock. Next, a big salad, not tossed, but with all separate vegetables on a plate, with a special kind of mild sauerkraut that was very tasty. Next came roast pork, Viennese style, [flavored with caraway seeds and juniper berries], tender and juicy in lots of gravy, with bread dumplings. For dessert she served peaches and ice cream, with Fini's own raspberry sauce. All served with red wine.

It was fantastic and we stuffed ourselves, prodded by her encouraging words to have a little more 'til we could hardly move. When we thought the meal was over, the piece de resistance arrived. Fini made us Apfelstrudel! Nobody would pass up this special homemade treat. It's a rare art to make Apfelstrudel in the old Viennese way and she certainly knew how to do it. It takes hours to make. And lots of effort, too. She said you have to slap the dough around hard for at least 15 minutes.

The entire meal lasted over three hours. Every one was visibly expanded around the middle. This "affliction" we referred to as a *Fini-bauch*, [Fini-paunch], after we left her house and waddled around to do some more sightseeing.

Gries Nockerln

Another Kind of Dumpling for Soup

Tante Fini in Vienna

Mom's Diary:

> We had a lot of confusion over the word *Gries* in
> the recipe, which we interpreted as "grease."
> Fini kept saying you add more *Gries* to make the
> dumplings firm.   We insisted "grease" would
> make them fall apart.   Finally, Fini cleared up
> this misunderstanding by bringing out a box of
> *Gries* from the kitchen.   It was farina!

1 egg, well beaten

Rampferl of salt – like, about a quarter or half a teaspoon

8 Kaffeeloeffeln Gries (8 t farina)

Beat everything well and let stand one hour.   Drop by
teaspoonfuls into boiling soup.   Cook covered 10 minutes.
Turn off heat and let stand in soup 10 minutes, covered.
Makes 10 *Nockerln* for any clear soup.

I love this word, *Nockerln*.   It's related to the Italian
gnocchi, which is a small potato dumpling.   Italians often eat
them with a sauce poured over them.   Domenico Tiepolo, in
quite a few of his *Pulcinella Drawings*, drew packs of
gluttonous Pulcinellas, congregating over a large pot of
gnocchi, which they are eagerly cooking up.

Egg Drop Soup

Chicken soup as above.   Then beat a farm egg or two and drop into soup a little at a time, without stirring.

Fanni and Johann, who liked his soup

Fanni's Liver Dumpling Soup

Codified by Mom

2 quarts beef broth, either homemade or canned or instant

½ lb liver

1 onion

2 farm eggs

3 T butter

¾ cup crumbs

2 T chopped parsley

½ tsp. marjoram

Salt and pepper to taste

Grind liver and onion together. Add all the rest of the ingredients to the liver and onion paste.   Fanni used a meat grinder, but you can use a food processor to grind and mix everything together. Form into a ball a little smaller than a golf ball. Drop into 2 quarts of broth and simmer for 10 minutes.

Makes about 1 to 2 dozen, depending on how small you make the dumplings.

Helen's Hearty Ginger Cabbage Soup

From Mom

For somebody who grew up hating soup, not to mention spices, the invention of this recipe is a miracle. Mom created this soup and it is just, truly wonderful!

In a large pot, saute one medium onion and 1 or 2 cloves of garlic in a little oil.

Add 5 or 6 cups water and bring to a boil, then turn down to simmer

Add 1 T dry veggie broth for each cup of water

Add 1 or 2 potatoes, diced

And 2 or 3 carrots sliced

And a medium head of cabbage, shredded

Season to taste with salt and pepper (red), seasoning salt (Mom uses a turmeric, paprika, celery, soy combo), and ginger (either 1 T freshly grated or 1 ½ tsp. dry).

Simmer the above for about 45 minutes, until the cabbage is soft.

Ladle into bowls and sprinkle chopped parsley in each one at the table, as a garnish.

My Mother

Mom's Lentil Soup

Mom hated this stuff, having grown up on it. But finally she came to enjoy lentils again with this recipe. She once made it for me and delivered it to my house when I was really down with the flu. That was the start of my cure – Mom and soup!

1 ½ cups lentils

1 large can of tomatoes, chopped

7 cups vegetable broth

2 or 3 medium onions, chopped

3 carrots, sliced

2 T extra virgin olive oil

1T vinegar

¾ tsp. marjoram

¾ tsp. thyme

salt and pepper to taste

Basically, you put everything in a pot and simmer for an hour and a half, until the lentils break apart.

Garnish with cup chopped fresh parsley and shredded cheddar cheese.

My Lentil Carrot Soup

One time I combined leftover lentil soup with left over carrot soup.   Oh boy! Was that ever good! You can do it this way for a really yummy, creamy soup.

Lentils - ¾ cup

Several cups of water, like 3 or 4

3 or 4 Cloves garlic, chopped

Red pepper to taste

Salt to taste

Put the above in a pot and cook 1 hour

After one hour, add to the pot:

Potato - one baker size or two mediums, cut up

1 Medium onion, chopped

4 Carrots, sliced

Simmer, with enough water to cover everything, for another 30 minutes, until the lentils start falling apart.   Then, put it in your food processor or blender, and add about 1 tsp. curry powder and buzz until pureed.

Get ready for some awesome soup!

Garnish with:

Chopped fresh tomatoes

Chopped Italian parsley

Olive oil drizzled over the garnishes

Mom chomping on a chicken bone

Fanni's passport picture at age 35

Chapter 3

Portrait of Fanni

Pentimento of Fanni's House

Portrait of Fanni

Throwing my arms around her waist to hug my Grandmother, when I was a little girl, was like melting into her. She was so big and soft. Her skin was soft, too, and papery and always felt warm to the touch. Clinging to it was the smell of roses, that came from Sweetheart soap and the chicken soup that always simmered away on her stove. When she laughed it was musical, like ice tinkling in a glass. German sounded pretty when she spoke it, with a soft, Viennese accent.

For everyday, Fanni wore a flowered cotton print dress and short bib apron. They both smelled freshly laundered and had been washed over the years to a thin, limp softness. She wore flesh-colored, cotton stockings that she held up with garters at the knee. Her cuban heeled oxfords made a dull clomp on her wooden floors, as she went about her work. Fanni was short and plump, but I eventually grew a half a foot taller, because I grew up drinking milk three times a day.

Fanni had polished apple cheeks, rosy and shiny, even though her face was always bare of makeup. Mom says that when she used to go out to dances, she'd put on a little rouge and face powder and stare at herself in the mirror. But I never saw that and I couldn't understand why she didn't go in for glamour, because I was fascinated watching my mother carefully paint on a full set of Hollywood lips. First Mom drew a careful border, way over her lip line, with a liner brush. Then she put on bright red lipstick and blotted that with powder to set it, and then applied another coat of lipstick over the top of that. I loved wearing lipstick when I played dress up, but I was only allowed to wear pink.

Fanni had the sweet, plain ways of the Austrian country girl she had been, before her father took her, at age 13, on the train to Vienna, to keep house for a family. "She had one personality for all occasions," my mother likes to say. Fanni was always cheerful, even in her later years when her aches and pains kept her in bed for the whole day. She had a pleasant, quiet way of radiating calm. And love. For a kid growing up in an alcoholic household, that was golden.

I always saw her treat everyone she knew with kindness. I admire that. Everyone got the same treatment – the grocer, the butcher, the baker that we met on her daily shopping rounds, her friends she would run into and chat with along the way, my entire family who gathered at her flat for dinner on Sundays, and even the stranger who rang the doorbell in a panic, after having a traffic accident out front on the busy street and needed to use the phone. Fanni saw people for who they were, not how they acted or what they did.

Yeah, except that one time when I heard her swear. She was sensitive about her neighborhood, which was on a downward slide by the time I came along, turning from a well tended German neighborhood into an absentee landlord slum. We were out doing the shopping, when she muttered under her breath, "Damned niggers!" Holy Cow! Just goes to show, she was human!

I heard her sing as she worked around her flat, doing the wash with a ringer washer and hanging clothes up on the line, cleaning, ironing, mending, gardening, cooking and making pillows in a cloud of feathers in the basement. Her idea of fun was playing cards with friends, having the family over for dinner, dancing to Viennese music at Wienerblut dances, and going on walks and picnicking along the way.

But sometimes Fanni seemed sad to me. By the time I knew her, she had outlived her four-year old son, her husband, her parents and most of her sisters and brothers. "Everyone I knew is dead," she would say, but never went into details. She would just sigh and say, "One day I'll get sick and then I'll have to die." My brother Robby thought that was morbid. But when I came home one fall, from my third year in college to visit her when she was in the hospital, she looked ashen. And when she said that again to me, I realized it might be the last time we would see each other. And it was.

So when her funeral came, I had been so well prepared that I smiled all the way through the Mass, feeling an overwhelming, inexplicable sense of joy, while everyone else was in tears. It was only the second funeral I had been to, but I knew smiling was out, so I kept turning down the corners of my mouth so as not to offend my family, who were all weeping and distraught, as you would expect. Good thing I had arrived late and missed the wake, because I wanted to remember her as a living, comforting, presence in my life. They were just closing the coffin, when my Dad brought me there from college and I saw her from way down the hallway.

Now that she was dead, I wasn't expecting that she would continue to provide that kind of comfort. But that's what happened, starting right then and there at her funeral, with that feeling of joy. After that, I started seeing her in my dreams, not as a character in them, but as a living presence. I began to feel her close by. Thoughts began to flit through my head, of being at Fanni's house, of standing in the dining room, playing under the window in the closet of her bedroom, sitting in the backyard, or going out and about doing the shopping with her. Even though it is now over 40 years since she crossed over, I still experience that pretty much every day.

Fanni's house on 20ᵗʰ and Highland

Pentimento – Grandma's House

I remember Fanni's house like I'd just come from there a few hours ago. It's a tranquil place, where impressions of the senses linger. Her real house was torn down in the mid 1960's, a casualty of urban renewal. But in my mind I can still hear the snap of the icebox latch catching, as the door clunked shut, and the *clomp, clomp, clomp* of Fanni's heavy footsteps on the old creaking wooden floors, as she walked from stove to table to ice box making something good to eat.

Fanni's house was a place where calm descends over everyone, and by everyone, I mean me and my brother Robby and my mother and father. We never fight there. Fanni has a gentle, pleasant nature and we all fall in line over at her house. My Mom describes her like this: "Mom had an indomitable spirit and kept the family on an even keel. She was always cheerful, no matter what the circumstances. She sang as she did her chores around the house. She had a pleasant, upbeat personality and an unassuming, sweet nature."

Dining Room

You hear the drum beat sound when someone walks up the steps onto the porch. That's how people in the house know someone is about to come in through the front door, which has a glass window etched with frost patterns, that rattles when you shut it.

The first room you enter is the dining room. That's where you can thaw out your backside against the radiator on a cold day. Right next to it is a big cabinet radio and above that is a picture of a goose girl. Next to that hangs a sentimental plaster bas relief painted in pastel colors of a little curly headed blonde girl, standing on her tip toes, sniffing low-hanging apple blossoms. In the center of the room is the handsome dining room table that Grandpa built. On the other side is a china cabinet he also built, with two long, tiny drawers. I stand on my tip toes as high as I can, so I can stretch my arm way up and fish out a colored pencil to draw with.

When my mother was a teenager, she was too embarrassed to bring her friends over to witness the homey scene taking place in the dining room. Her father, Johann and their boarder Uncle Herman, both out of work, would be sitting on either side of the table in their sleeveless undershirts. While reading the German newspaper, Johann might be paring an apple and bringing the knife with the slice on it to his mouth with his thumb, or perhaps scooping bacon drippings out of a old can and spreading it on a piece of rye bread. On the other side of the table, Uncle Herman smoked a cigar, while soaking stamps in a little dish of water, picking them up with a tweezers, laying them on a dry cloth, and placing them into a big stamp book, which lay open before him.

Fanni sat at the far end of the dining room table, by the kitchen, where she sprinkled clothes, knitted mittens, darned the family's socks, embroidered pillow cases, and kept her account books for the household. All the while they were sitting around the dining room table, they spoke to each other in German. Apparently, my teenage mother never saw the glamorous people in movies acting like this. *Ach du lieber!*

Postcards from Sitzgras, where Fanni came from.

Now in the Czech Republic

On cloudy days a single, lonely bulb from the chandelier over the dining room table shines in the gloom. Fanni's lower flat is sandwiched so tightly between two other houses, that even on the brightest days, only a thin light filters in through the cotton lace curtains hanging over the windows.

I talk to Fanni while she knits in the dining room. She is seated on the chair closest to the window so she can see well, making a pair of mittens with four needles. I ask Fanni to show me how to knit with four, but she goes so fast, I can't get it.

Grandma and I eat treats there in the dining room when we are alone together – things we picked up earlier that day from the bakery - crullers rolled in granulated sugar that crunch against my teeth and frosted long johns so fresh, the frosting is still soft. Sometimes we eat Hershey bars there, breaking off one square at a time and letting it melt slowly in our mouths. As a special treat, Fanni gives me 7 Up to drink, which somehow fizzes out my nose after I've swallowed it. Boy does that hurt.

Fanni drinks coffee with milk out of her white cup with the border of purple grape leaves on it, that says, "Mom." She makes coffee with an old, drip coffee maker, but sometimes, she also makes it right in the pan. First, she boils the water, then she throws ground coffee in the pan, lets it sit a few minutes, and pours it into her cup with a strainer. Finally, she adds lots of milk or cream. Usually she gives me milk to drink, but sometimes I ask Fanni for coffee. She makes it for me by pouring a *schlook* of coffee in another grape ringed cup. Then she fills the rest of the cup with warm milk and stirs in some sugar. "That's not coffee!" I protest.

"Yah! Coffee fur Kind!" is her reply. Warm milk with a little coffee actually sounds pretty good to me, now.

Kitchen

Fanni's kitchen is narrow, because it had been a pantry before the house was converted into a duplex and her bedroom used to be the kitchen. Along the wall a cast iron, Roper gas stove stands on legs three feet high. Underneath our beagle likes to loaf so she can soak up heat and keep an eye on tidbits that fall to the floor. "It was a big improvement over the wood stove on 16th Street," my mother recalls, "which had to be carefully watched so it didn't overheat the food." It has an eye level oven on the right, and the top is handy for keeping cooked foods warm or warming up plates. On the left of the oven sit four gas burners with white porcelain handles. Above those is an iron shelf where Fanni keeps the few spices she used regularly – salt, pepper, and cinnamon. I like to sit under the stove too, on a blanket, and watch Fanni go back and forth while she cooks.

In the middle of the narrow room is the wooden kitchen table Grandpa built, standing in front of the single window, where Fanni prepares food. Sometimes we eat breakfast there, too, sitting on bentwood chairs Johann also made, whose spindles always poke me in the back. I finally learned how to sit comfortably in a bentwood, about 20 years later, by placing my backbone between the rungs. That's when I was in art school and I got some used ones, painted them and put them in my kitchen. Against the other long wall in Fanni's kitchen is a big sink. Next to it is the long red and white what-not cabinet, with all kinds of cupboards and drawers, that Johann built for all her cooking stuff. Other

Fanni, bentwood chair, Mom in 16th St. backyard

interesting items are kept in there, too, things I like to play with, like a wad of string I like to unravel and roll up into a ball, and a ball made of rubber bands that doesn't bounce very well.

Bathroom

Before bedtime, I climb into her high bathtub with the ball and claw feet. I have to stand on a wooden a stool while Fanni holds my elbow to steady me. During the day, the room is so dark, I have to leave the door open for light when I tinkle, because I can't reach the hanging light pull. Sometimes a shaft of light falls between the narrow space between Fanni's house and the one next door, and paints a slice of light on the glass. But now at night, the smooth porcelain handles on the bathtub gleam from the overhead bulb that hangs in a bell shaped glass shade. The spigot whines as it spurts out warm water. A little metal wire basket hangs over the edge of the tub, holding an oval bar of Sweetheart soap, which Fanni picks up and rubs onto a washcloth, worn thin from being washed for decades. I sit in a couple of inches of water, as she rubs me down, wondering what it would be like to soak in such a big, tall tub, if I could ever convince Fanni to fill the huge tub to the rim with hot water.

Bedroom

In Grandma's bedroom, the fluffy feather bed levitates like a cloud over the iron bed, waiting to enfold us, when we climb in at night. I love Fanni's big double bed. In my house, my parents just have twin beds with ordinary store-bought woolen comforters. When I climb up and burrow under Fanni's cozy feather bed, I look in the tilted beveled glass mirror of Grandma's pretty dresser and see the wooden floor boards, running diagonally. I watch Grandma shuffle around her bedroom in her sleeping shift, with mules on her feet, going through her goodnight routine. She opens the window a few inches to let in the fresh night air. The Big Ben alarm clock gets wound up with a loud rasping sound. Fanni gets on her knees and puts it under the bed, where it ticks off the seconds like something alive. The wooden floor it sits on acts like a drum, amplifying the striking of every second. While Fanni is down there, she says her prayers. Then she slips off her mules, which she puts next to the clock under the bed, turns off the light switch on the wall, and climbs into the bed in the dark.

Sometimes I wake up in the middle of the night. I lie awake there under the feather bed, transfixed by the loud ticking of the clock under the bed. Patterns of lace, and the faint mosaic of old glass, shine on the walls from car headlights out on the street, and slide silently along the walls in the darkness. Fanni is sleeping next to me. But she has become transformed into a fairy tale giant, shaking the bed with her loud snoring. The periodic rhythm of her snores stop and there is silence. Then she gasps and struggles for air. And her snoring continuezzzzzzzzzzzz.

In the morning, the Big Ben alarm under the bed rings loud enough to be heard way down the street. Fanni throws back the feather bed, gets down on her knuckles and knees on the floor, and reaches under the bed for the clock so she can punch the alarm button in. Now she is cheerful and smiling. Fanni beacons me to get out of bed, as she puts the clock in its daytime location, on the dresser. She comes back and helps me down from the big bed. Then she peels the feather bed, with all its warmth, back to the foot of the bed, walks over to the window and throws it open wide, no matter what the temperature. Air and sunlight burst in.

I stand on tip toes, trying to see my reflection in the tilted beveled mirror on the dresser, but I can only see the tops of the windows and the shadows painted by the light, in the angles the walls make with the ceiling. Sometimes someone knocks on the door next to her treadle sewing machine and the rocker. It startles me, because I am so used to the door not opening. Fanni unlocks the hook on the door and has a conversation with Mrs. Karl, her renter upstairs. You can always hear the comforting sound of Mrs. and Mr. Karl's footfalls upstairs, treading on the wooden floor.

In the Depression, a Mrs. Gnerich lived there with her teenage children Udine and Erik. She did alterations for a high end crowd. Fanni liked her because she paid steady rent. Her husband lived in an "insane asylum," which he escaped from periodically and made his way to their upstairs flat. That's when Fanni locked the doors to the house and told my Mom, who was a child, to stay inside and not go out. Mrs. Gnerich had to call the police to come and take her husband back.

When my parents drop me and my brother Robby off at Fanni's for a couple of days, they tell us, "Don't leave the yard or go out to the street or the alley without Grandma. And whatever you do, *never, ever, ever* go kitty corner across the street to play with the girls at the 'Home for Wayward Girls.'" I used to watch them play outside from across the street. I wondered if they hadn't listened to their parents and were sent away for being disobedient. A few years ago, I stopped by Grandma's old neighborhood and found the current owner painting the old Home for Wayward Girls. He had purchased the mansion some years before, and was restoring it bit by bit.

"Do you remember if there was a stained glass window downstairs?"

I thought a moment. "Yeah," I replied, "there was one with panes of different colored glass around this big, bay window here." Just cause I couldn't go there, didn't mean I didn't look!

Backyard

Fanni and I take the cream colored, bentwood kitchen chairs outside on a warm day and sit in them on the grass, where we hand sew and embroider in the fresh air. The warm sun shines down on us, as I thread needles for her and learn how to make fancy stitches, like French knots. Fanni embroiders her own pillowcases, following designs that had been stamped on them when she bought them at the dime store. She also tats scalloped borders on them, but when she leans over to show me how to do it, I can't figure it. Finally, some years after Fanni was gone, I did learn, from a lady in my neighborhood, so I could finish some pillowcases Fanni had started.

I like to keep Fanni company when she uses the wringer washer, which I am not allowed to touch. I like helping her hang the clothes out to dry in the backyard. I am too short to reach the line, so I hand Fanni the clothes pins. The lace curtains that hang over all the windows in the house for privacy, also have their day in the backyard. She washes them in the basement by hand and then stretches them on a rack outside, so they keep their shape as they dry.

Fanni with the wash on 16ᵗʰ Street

I try to beat the woolen carpets when she hangs them on the line, but I don't raise much dust with the carpet beater. With her hair covered, Fanni whacks them with a carpet beater, that has curlicues of heavy wire mounted in a wooden handle. She sends a big cloud of dust flying up into the air. The wind mysteriously carries it away.

That's what the dust cap was for. I never actually saw Fanni wear any kind of frilly dust cap, like the one I found in a box of crocheted stuff, she gave to me when she moved out of her house in the 1960's. I found a picture of one like it in a vintage hat book and learned it was from the 20's. There were other curious things in that box, too, like a breast pump made of glass and rubber, an old clock that didn't run, and a wooden desk calendar, which I remember sat on top of the desk Grandpa had made. It had three windows in front, that each had rollers on the side, where you changed the day, month and year. Now we would think that was ecological.

Basement

Our beagle Thumper loves Grandma's basement, especially the coal bin where she likes to bury her bones. After a while, Mom realizes Thumper has disappeared and finds her rooting around in the coal bin, with charcoal gray paws. Much to Thumper's dislike, Mom cleans her paws off with a washrag and soap. I don't know what all the fuss is about. Given the chance, our dog would lick herself clean like a cat. But Fanni's house is so clean. I guess my Mom doesn't want to mess it up. The truth is, Fanni is really a lot more tolerant of things, than Mom is. Like one time, when I was jumping on her sofa, I put my foot through a pink ruffled pillow and begged her not to tell Mom. She didn't and the next time I came, Fanni had fixed that pillow, so you couldn't tell anything had ever happened. She never spanks us, either, like our parents do.

The basement is also a workplace, where Fanni does her canning on a low wood stove in the main room. There is a little room down there, where you can look out under the front porch, where the wooden cupboard with the stuff Fanni canned is. When you open it, there were the Ball jars all lined up on the shelves, stuffed with voluptuous shapes like tomato wedges with their rows of seeds exposed and peaches looking spooky under the blue glass of canning jars.

Fanni does laundry down there, which in the old days had to be cooked in a copper boiler. Sometimes when Mom was a girl, she'd see bloody towels soaking in cold water down in the basement. When she asked Fanni about it, she was told, "Dad had another nose bleed." Those were really the towels Fanni and Margaret used in their undies every month. Mom was kept completely in the dark, so she thought something terrible was wrong with her, when she got her first period.

I remember seeing Fanni down there, one time, in one of those little rooms, working on a pillow on her lap, with little feathers floating in the air and feathers stuck to her hairnet. She was shaving the feathers with a knife and stuffing them back into the pillow. That's how she recycled those feathers when they became brittle and poked through the casing. She had also made her featherbed, *and* shaved it, two monumental tasks!

Icebox

Johann had built her a hanging pantry on the stairs to the basement, an unheated part of the house. That was her only way to keep things cool when they first lived there. When I was a kid, Fanni had an icebox, so that hanging pantry was a dark, cool place where she kept goodies. Sometimes I tip toe back there and slide the plate back from the crock where she keeps the cookies, reach inside and grab a few.

The icebox was on the landing on the back steps to the basement. Ice cream wouldn't stay frozen in it, so the drug store was the only place you could get ice cream. Once or twice a week, the iceman would come traipsing through the house, hefting a big block of ice with a huge tongs. These chunks were carved out of a monster wall of ice, which had been removed from a river or lake in the winter, and stored in a warehouse all summer until it was time to go into the delivery truck. She had to keep an eye on her ice box so the drip pan didn't spill over. Because then she'd have to mop up the back steps all the way down to the basement with a rag, wrapped around a long wooden stick with a "T" on the end of it.

Living Room

Sometimes Fanni puts me down for a nap on the love seat in the living room, under the etching. She pulls the shades low and closes the double pocket doors. I am alone with the old elegant furniture, with its graceful curves. In the summer, I hear the rhythmic creak of the front porch swing through the open window and the low murmur of voices, intermittently drowned out by the roar of traffic, when the stoplight changes.

I look up at that etching hanging from the picture rail until I fall asleep. One day, Fanni came across it at Schuster's Department store and had to have it. They didn't have the money for such things, but she bought it with her household money, hard-earned cash she made doing other people's laundry and cleaning. It must have taken her a long time of scrimping, to make up that deficit! Signed by Emile Le Comte, the tinted etching depicts a house in the French countryside, surrounded by a stucco wall. A man walks up to a door in the wall, with a large bundle slung over his back. Le Comte's editions of similarly peaceful scenes turned up in a lot of department stores in America, because I saw another one at a boyfriend's parent's house in Philadelphia.

One time when I was in Florence, Italy, I shared a park bench with a couple of elderly ladies from Austria, sunning themselves on a January day. I told them the story of how Fannie bought the etching. "Oh yes!" they exclaimed earnestly. "That's typically Austrian, spending your food money on art. Beauty is very important!"

I have that settee and etching in my house. I can still feel like I am at Grandma's, when curl up on the settee and look up at the etching.

Art: definitely worth the grocery money

*Johann, Herman, Fanni, Mom & Johnny
picnicking at Devil's Lake*

Chapter 4

Veggie Dishes

Fresh Bean Salad

Reconstructed by Mom

Green and yellow beans, blanched and cut

Raw, thinly sliced onion

For the dressing:

White vinegar

Oil

Sugar

Crumbled bacon

Green and yellow beans, blanched.

Mix together white vinegar, oil and sugar. Dress beans.

Add raw chopped onions. Chill a while to cool beans.

Top with crumbled bacon right before serving.

Potato Salad

Boiled red potatoes, peel and cut into slices

[Good way to use up left over potatoes]

For the dressing:

White vinegar

Oil

A little sugar

Crumbled bacon

Salt and black pepper to taste

Cut left over potatoes into slices.

Mix vinegar and oil and sugar. Add salt and black pepper to taste. Pour dressing over potatoes. Add crumbled bacon and toss lightly.

Cucumber Salad

Codified by Mom

3 cucumbers

1-2 tsp. sugar

½ tsp. salt

1 T salad oil

3 T vinegar

Peel and slice thin about 3 cucumbers. Crisp a while in cold water. Drain well. Whisk together dressing of 1 or 2 tsp. sugar, ½ tsp. salt, 1 T salad oil and 3 T vinegar. Pour over cucumbers and mix together. Chill.

Johnny, Mom, Johann, Fanni at Devil's Lake

Burpless Cucumber Salad with Sour Cream

from Margaret

Cucumber

Salt

2 or 3 T of sour cream or low fat yogurt

Peel and slice thin. Place in a bowl and salt slices. About a half hour later, drain off liquid. Dress with sour cream. You can substitute low fat yogurt.

Simple but tasty. Refreshing on a hot day when you don't feel like eating anything.

Johann, Johnny, Mom & Fanni at Devil's Lake

Red Cabbage

A Sweet and Sour Dish

An Austrian classic codified by Mom

1 small head of red cabbage

½ cup water

1 T oil

2 tsp. sugar

1 tsp. salt

1 T flour

2 T vinegar

cloves

Shred small head of red cabbage. Put in a pan and add a ½ cup, or a little more, of water. Use water sparingly.

Add 1 T oil, 2 tsps. sugar, 1 tsp. salt. Cook covered about 10 minutes until tender.

Make a paste with 1 T flour and a little water. Stir into cabbage. Add 2 T vinegar and some cloves. Cook about 5 minutes more to blend flavors.

Add more salt, sugar or vinegar to taste if necessary.

Vegetables with Toasted Bread Crumbs

Reconstructed by Mom

veggies, like cauliflower, brussels sprouts or asparagus

butter or olive oil

½ cup or more of breadcrumbs

First, in a skillet, brown about half a cup or more of breadcrumbs in butter or oil, such as extra virgin olive oil. Fanni boiled her veggies until soft, but you can steam cauliflower, brussels sprouts or asparagus, (or all three) to your liking. Watch the breadcrumbs as they toast, so they don't burn.

Place cooked veggies in a bowl and sprinkle on crunchy bread crumbs.

The best bread crumbs for this come from old Kaiser rolls, really hard rolls if you can find them. Otherwise, try a French baguette.

Einbrenn

This is a sauce for veggies, like cauliflower, kohlrabi or peas & carrots. For gluten free, you could substitute almond meal, or the meal of another nut, for the flour.

2 T Lard, [substitute butter or cold pressed oil]

2 T Flour [or substitute nut meal]

Salt and Pepper

Cooked Veggies

[For carrots, cut carrots into small cubes]

Drained veggie water or plain water

Cook veggies with steam or by boiling. Melt the fat in a separate frying pan at medium. Turn heat to low. Add enough flour to make a smooth paste, thinning it with either water or the water from cooking the veggies, until you have a mixture with a creamy consistency. Add salt and pepper to taste. Then add the cooked veggies to the sauce in the pan and sauté a few minutes, stirring, to coat the veggies.

Kohlrabi

Reconstructed by Mom

Young kohlrabis, cubed

Milk or sour cream

Water

Salt and Pepper

Flour to make paste

Cube kohlrabi and simmer in half milk or sour cream, with half water, and salt and pepper, until tender.

Make a paste with flour and a little of the milk-and-water mixture in a separate cup.

Gradually add the flour mixture to the main pot and return to stove, heating until the sauce thickens.

Boiled Potatoes

Wash and peel small or medium red potatoes

Boil in water until tender

Nothing special about these, but they are really good with any kind of gravy. Fanni also served them with crumbled bacon and butter.

Pan Roasted Potatoes

from Renate in Vienna

2 lbs boiled or baked potatoes
¼ cup of lard [substitute butter or cold pressed oil]
¼ cup bacon
½ cup chopped onion
Salt and a little butter

Boil, potato peel, and chop. Heat the lard in a frying pan, fry finely chopped onion and bacon in it.   Mix in potatoes, season with salt.

Melt butter and add to the potatoes and fry until crisp.

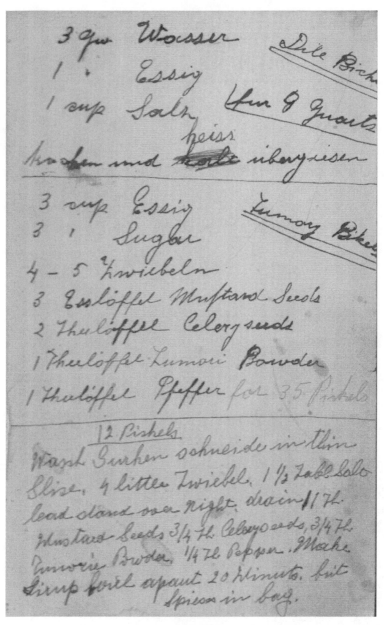

Fanni's Pickle Recipes

Pickles

from Fanni

Fanni had three recipes for pickles written by hand in the back of a Rumford cookbook. She made spiced pickles, dill pickles, and sweet pickles. All three variations are included here.

Spiced Pickles

12 Cucumbers

4 small onions, chopped

1 ½ T salt

Wash gurkens and cut into thin slices. Combine with 4 little onions, chopped and 1 ½ T salt. Let stand overnight. Drain. Put the drained cucumber slices into sterilized jars.

Put white vinegar, or half vinegar and water into a pan. You want enough to be able to cover your pickles in jars. This depends on the size of your cukes and your jars

Add the following spices, in a cloth bag, to the vinegar:

1 t mustard seed

¾ t celery seed

¾ t turmeric powder

¼ t pepper

Then add 1/3 cup of sugar.

Boil the spice, sugar and vinegar mixture for about 20 minutes in a non-aluminum pan. Take out the bag of spices. Pour the hot "syrup" over the cucumber slices and seal while hot. Process the packed jars for 10 minutes in a boiling water bath.

Dill Pickles

For dill pickles, follow the spiced pickle recipe, but skip the spices and sugar and replace with 2 ½ tsp. dill.

Sweet Pickles

Found this recipe in the Rumford book, in Mom's writing. Betty remembers these were called "Slippery Jims"

1 doz. ripe cucumbers

3 lbs sugar

1 qt. vinegar

2 T mustard seeds

stick cinnamon

1 T cloves, heads removed.

Peel cucumbers. Cut in two lengthwise, scrape out seeds with a silver spoon. Salt and let stand overnight. Drain and dry cucumbers. Make a syrup of the sugar and vinegar. Add the mustard seeds, and also the whole cinnamon and cloves, tied in a bag. Boil cucumbers in this syrup only until they are glassy. They must remain crisp. Pack in jars and cover air-tight. Can as usual.

Iceberg Salad

Remember when salad was just a plain affair? Start by crisping the lettuce for a half hour in cold water. Drain. Tear iceberg lettuce into pieces.

Whisk together a little oil, a little less vinegar and a little sugar to taste. Pour over lettuce just before serving.

When I was a little kid, the taste of vinegar was too strong for me, so Grandma used to sprinkle a little sugar over my salad.

Contrary to popular belief, iceberg lettuce does actually have nutrients. And it's a raw food. It's also refreshing to eat on a hot day, because it's crispy and has a high water content.

Fanni cozying up to Dad at Devil's Lake

My Green Salad

Purely my own invention

½ head romaine, shredded

1 package or 4 oz misticanza, i.e. mixed baby greens

sliced mushrooms

sliced red peppers

1 jar marinated artichoke hearts

shredded red cabbage

thinly slice carrots

green onions

balsamic vinegar

olive oil

salt and red pepper

garlic clove, finely chopped

raw sunflower seeds

optional avocado

This makes a visual feast as well as a yummy salad. Mix above ingredients together and toss. Then sprinkle raw sunflower seeds over the top. Add any other veggies you are fond of and have on hand, like fresh tomatoes.

Italian dressing

I have seen my Italian friend Manuela dress a salad this way many times. Using your first two fingers as a drizzle spout over the opening of the bottle, sprinkle extra virgin olive oil over the salad. Then do the same with balsamic vinegar. Sprinkle finely chopped garlic, and salt and red pepper over the salad and toss lightly.

Avocado Dressing

Mash a ripe avocado and put in a small bowl. Add olive oil, balsamic vinegar, finely chopped garlic, and salt and red pepper to it, and mix. Pour over salad and toss.

Two Sisters - Margaret and Mom at Lake Park in Milwaukee

Horseradish Sauce

Horseradish root, finely grated

Oil and vinegar to make a paste with the horseradish

Sat and pepper to taste

Fanni's husband Johann made it, with horseradish root that Johnny, Margaret's husband, grew, according to Mom's recollection.

When the root was harvested, Johann grated it on a fine grater. He added a little oil and salt and pepper and vinegar to it to make a hot, pungent spread, which he put on rye bread, instead of butter.

Johann had a penchant for strong tastes. He also used to eat Limburger cheese, a particularly stinky cheese. My mother didn't like the smell at all and left the table when her Dad was eating it.

My Grandpa, Johann, and me

Chapter 5

Johann

The Summerhouse

Johann

Johann secretly did the work of Santa Claus on Christmas Eve, when we all went down to Fanni's house to celebrate. When we got there, we went into the living room to admire the tree in front of the windows, trimmed with ornaments and tinsel, but no lights. Those came later. Pretty soon, we all crowded into the dining room and someone pushed in the button that turned off the living room lights and the room went dark. The heavy, sliding pocket doors were pulled closed.

Then, we waited for Santa. While I was waiting, I tried to remember that Santa was on his way, so I could dash through the pocket doors into the living room, as soon as we heard the sound of sleigh bells, and catch a glimpse of him riding away with his reindeer. But I always got distracted talking to people and playing with stuff and pretty soon it slipped my mind.

After about an hour of waiting, someone would call out, "Listen!" And we would hear the muffled jingling of sleigh bells in the front room. My brother and I flew to the pocket doors and tried to pry them apart with our fingers, but they were so heavy we couldn't get them to move. By the time one of the grown ups rolled the doors back, and we ran in to see if we could catch sight of Santa climbing out the porch window, he always managed to have disappeared.

But then we were awed by the sight of the Christmas tree glowing in the dark, that Santa had festooned with multicolored lights. The pile of gaily wrapped packages he left for us underneath the tree was like a magnet, and we immediately rushed to them and began reading the labels and handing them out. I have those sleigh bells that Johann rang

Christmas with Fanni, Mom, Margaret and friend

Johann, also known as Santa Claus

from the porch hanging on my front door knob. They're on a leather harness that still has a black shoe lace tied to it, because that's how Johann used to ring the bells from the porch, right before he made his getaway into the house. After Grandpa passed away, Johnny, Margaret's husband did Santa's routine.

Johann fixed stuff and did the outside work around the house. He cut the grass with a push mower. After he died, Uncle Herman did the grass. At our house I used to help my Dad with the push mover, my hands outstretched before me on the wooden handles. I ran along side him laughing, as the blades whirled, spitting grass up in the air. At Fanni's I was just supposed to stay out of the way. Then when Uncle Herman died, finally there was just Fanni left to cut the grass. I used to watch my Grandmother in her 70's drag her mower up the steep slope of her front yard and push it back down again.

Johann did the gardening, too. He built a rock garden near the house, on a little shady slope in the back, with succulents and tiny flowers spilling over the cool rocks. He also planted the narrow flowerbeds along the neighbor's wire fence, with long, tall blue bachelor buttons and pink cosmos, with feathery leaves. Next to them, he planted a patch of zinnias that bloomed in a riot of colors. Even after he had gone, these beds of annuals always came back in the same place, because they reseeded themselves. Perhaps that was because they had been so well manured.

According to my mother, Grandpa went out into the street with his shovel, to scoop up manure dropped by a passing horse pulling a wagon. Then he'd bring his poop-laden shovel to the backyard and spread fresh manure on his little gardens. Fanni admonished him, "Why do you have to

Me and Dad mowing the lawn

do that? All the neighbors can see you shoveling up *haufis*" [a euphemism for turds, literally meaning "a pile of something"]

"You do your work, I do mine," he grumbled.

Like Grandma, Grandpa didn't go to church. But he had an entirely different reason. Mom explains, "Grandpa despised the church, after his experiences in the Great War." He was a spotter in a machine gun trio, along with two other soldiers who operated the gun. When he was shot in the leg, Mom says, "He didn't get any help from the Red Cross or from doctors. He was just left to die after being wounded. He made his way, without any help, back to Vienna on his injured leg, which by this time had turned gangrene. He saved his own life by cutting out the gangrene with his pocket knife."

When my Mom was a kid, sometimes the nuns came by and rang the bell, with the idea in mind to convince Johann to come to church. "He was reading the paper at the dining room table," Mom explains, "when Fanni answered the door and let them in. He would tell them to leave. *'And don't ever come back!'* he would say. They always came back another day to try to persuade him again."

Basically, neither Fanni nor Johann went to Mass. So Mom didn't go to church, either. But when Mom was nine, Margaret, her older sister by ten years, had a talk with Fanni and convinced her that Mom should go to catechism. Mom says, "My sister bossed me around and took me places and made me behave the way she thought I ought to do. Fanni didn't interfere."

Johann passed away when I was just 1½ years old. But I remember a game Grandpa and I used to play in the last year of his life, out in front of their house, on the sidewalk. We put little wooden milk bottles in the wooden wagon Johann had made, and pulled the wagon, rattling on its wooden wheels, down the sidewalk. We dropped the bottles off on the front steps at each of the neighbor's. Then we'd go back and pick up the "empties." When we played that game he was dying, cared for at home by Fanni.

Johann working in the garden

The Summer House

Johann built an octagon summer house in the back yard. I really loved that place. He built it with scrap wood he had collected from out on the streets and alleys, and from pieces that friends had saved for him. That's how he got the wood for all his carpentry projects: salvage. At the time he built the summer house, he couldn't work inside, because he was suffering from asthma.

Clinging to the outside of the summer house, were dark green, leafy, wild grape vines, growing over the latticework outside the window screens. The vines were so thick that even on a hot day, it was dark and cool inside. The leaves spread themselves out flat against the screens, radiating a soothing, green light through their translucent leaves, that highlighted their opaque veins. The vines sent out tiny suction cup fingers, that grabbed onto the mesh of the screens.

In the penumbra of the interior, a day bed was laid with a pink and maroon, striped floral spread. It sat ready for the next inhabitant to sink into it with a squeaking of springs and take a snooze under the stained glass window. The window glowed in the dark interior like jewels, with its square panes of blue, red, yellow and green. It was another item Johann had saved from a demolition site. A trundle bed was tucked under the day bed, ready to be pulled out for another sleeper. Dangling from the octagonal star of the roof rafters was a coconut on a string, an exotic gift to Margaret from an admirer.

Johann relaxing on the swing he built in the back yard

The summerhouse covered in grape leaves

The skeleton key to this little sanctuary was hidden on a ledge above the door. Of course, that's where you would look for it, but even the big house was never locked in my Mom's day, except when they went away. My mother and her sister Margaret played games out there, and sometimes they carried their meals out there, too, and ate by themselves. On warm nights they slept out there. A small hook and eye lock on the screen door was all they needed to keep them safe overnight. During the winter, the two sisters slept on the creaky living room couch, that they unfolded nightly with a groaning of springs, into a double bed.

When I was little, just a decade after my mother's childhood, a ghetto had grown up around Fanni's and we couldn't spend any nights out in the summerhouse. When Grandma's house was slated for demolition in an urban renewal project in the 60's, the city paid her considerably less than the house and property was actually worth. I wanted to have the summer house moved to our house, but the idea didn't capture my parents' imagination. I wanted Mom to have Grandma move in with us, but she told me, "there's too much turmoil in this house for Grandma to be happy here."

So Fanni moved to a big, elderly housing project not too far away, in the inner city. Mom says she liked her little apartment there, because it was small and easy to keep up, compared to the big duplex. Then one day, when Fanni was on her way to the store, a neighborhood kid looking for easy money pushed her down on the ground and took her purse. She was bruised, but okay. I felt really helpless. After that when she went shopping, she only carried a little knit bag that I made for her, hanging from her wrist on a ribbon.

Grandpa on the front steps on 20th St.

This is how good Johann's Root Beer made my Mom feel

Chapter 6

Beverages

Grape Juice

Copied from Fanni's handwriting

10 lbs. Grapes

2 lbs. sugar

2 quarts water

Use only ripe Grapes. Pick and wassh grapes. Plase in kettle, cover with the water und let boil until seeds are free. Strain while hot through bag. Heat juice to boiling point und skim. Let boil up again und skim. Den add sugar. Heat to boiling point 1 Minute. Pour into sterilized Jars and Seal.

I love the way Fanni mixes phonetic spelling and German with standard English! I can just imagine what my poor German looks like, when I email my cousins in Vienna!

10 lb Grapes   2 lb sugar   2 quarts Water

Use only ripe Grapes pick and wash grapes
Place in kettle cover with the water and
let boil until seeds are free. Strain while
hot through bag Heat juice to boiling
point and skim Let boil up again
and skim, then add sugar
Heat to boiling point boil 5 Minute.
Pour into sterilized Jars and seal

(Grape Juice)

Fanni's recipe for Grape Juice

Root Beer

Mom remembers her father Johann making root beer in the basement. He would make up a batch and pour it off into bottles. It was a big treat when he would bring some up from the cellar and they sipped it through hollow pasta straws. You can still get hollow pasta to use as a straw today – it's called *bucatini*.

We think of root beer, and other soft drinks like Coke, Pepsi, and Dr. Pepper, as recreational drinks. But originally these were tonics made from medicinal herbs. They were brewed with yeast and sugar and bottled to produce carbonation. A look at an old ingredient list from a 1922 pamphlet by Hires Root Beer shows that a host of medical herbs went into their formula: Birch Bark, Dog Grass, Ginger, Juniper Berries, Licorice, Wintergreen, Chirreta, Ginger, Hops, Licorice, Sarsasparilla, Vanilla, and Yerba Mate. Today soft drinks are just made with extracts, which may or may not actually contain herbs.

How did Johann make it? Did he buy an extract, add yeast and sugar and pour it off into his own bottles? Or did he gather his own roots and make it that way? My guess is he did the total DIY approach, because making something from scratch was how Fanni and Johann did things. And it was economical. Many root beer plants are not only traditional Native American herbs, but also sturdy prairie plants that grow as weeds in backyards, such as dandelion and burdock.

DIY Rootbeer

Make a concoction of herbs and roots. Add sweetener and yeast. Ferment and bottle.

Bottling is tricky, so please consult a website for more information on doing it right. Terafan Greydragon, a Society for Creative Anachronism member, has some terrific ideas on brewing root beer, with some tasty recipes:

http://www.greydragon.org/library/brewing_root_beer.html

Quickie Rootbeer

Use an herbal extract, sweetener and seltzer.

Check out this website where you can purchase an extract to combine with a sweetener and seltzer to make root beer. www.homemadesodacompany.com

Dr. Chase's 1869 Recipe for Medicinal Root Beer

If you know anything about herbs, you can see that this recipe is basically a spring tonic, whose purpose was to detoxify the blood.

For each gallon of water take hops, burdock, yellow dock, sarsaparilla, dandelion and spikenard roots, bruised, of each ½ oz. Boil about 20 min, and strain while hot. Add 8-10 drops of oils of spruce and sassafras [oops – the sale of sassafras was outlawed by the U.S. Government in 1960, as carcinogenic after experiments with some unfortunate lab rats] mixed in equal proportions. When cooled to a warm temp add 2-3 T yeast, molasses 2/3 pint, or white sugar ½ lb. Put the mix into a jar, with a cloth covering it, let it work for 2-3 hrs, then bottle and set in a cool place.

Remember to look up bottling advice on the web so the bottles don't explode.

Coffee

Fanni made coffee with an old style drip pot. But sometimes, she just made it right in the pan, something I learned to do as a grown up, from her.

I remember that Grandma had a coffee grinder, with a hand crank. *Grrrrr*. Meanwhile she boils the water, then throws the coffee, which she has freshly ground, into the pan. She lets it sit a few minutes. Then she pours it into her cup through a strainer and adds lots of milk or cream – several tablespoonfuls.

Usually she gives me milk to drink, but sometimes I ask Fanni for coffee. She makes it for me in another grape ringed cup, by pouring a *schlook* of coffee in the cup, and filling the rest of the cup with warm milk and stirring in some sugar. "That's not coffee!" I protest.

"Ja! Coffee fur Kind!" is her reply. It actually sounds pretty good to me now, because I like the flavor of coffee, but not the jolt.

Coffee Recipe

Bring two cups of water to a boil to make 2 cups of coffee. Remove from heat. Add one scoop of coffee – more or less, depending on how strong or weak you like your coffee. Let stand a few minutes. Strain directly into your coffee cup with a small strainer. Add your choice of milk, cream and sweetener. You can also put whipped cream in your coffee, something people did at dessert time at Fanni's.

Coffee fur Kind

Put a schlook of coffee in a cup – like, about 1 or 2 T. Fill the rest of the cup with warm milk. Stir in sugar.

Homemade Grape Wine

Mom recalls: "For wine making, my father made a big wooden tub, bigger and higher than a wash tub, with a metal lining. Fanni went to the farmers market on 17th and Fond du Lac, with the red coaster wagon, and came back with the wagon loaded with boxes of concord grapes. "

"My Dad made the wine in his big wooden tub, using it like a big mortar. He didn't do it like the Italians, with their feet. He used a big wooden mallet. It took an awful lot of pounding with that mallet," my mother recalls. "It was like a sledge hammer, but flatter, so he could mash the grapes, to make mushed grapes and juice. The hammer was pretty heavy and he made it in his workshop, just like he made all his tools." That includes the mallet he made for Fanni to pound Wiener Schnitzel.

He made red wine and bottled it in glass bottles. And he made it during Prohibition, when it was illegal to make even your own wine at home. But nobody thought anything of it! Mom says the grape juice left over from wine making was "delicious." We don't know his exact recipe, but now you know his technique for mashing grapes.

Fanni used to keep a bottle of Mogen David Grape Wine in the back of her fridge for guests. During my childhood, sometimes Fanni could be convinced to have a single glass of wine from the bottle of Mogen David. She poured out about an ounce into a special little aperitif glass and drank it straight down all at once, laughing, "Ja, that's the way I always do it!"

Sometimes I was allowed a sip, too, but just a sip. It was sticky sweet, with a weird bite to it. I couldn't imagine why anyone would want to drink it.

Johann on the back yard swing he made

Lemonade

1 cup sugar

6 cups water

half a dozen lemons – about 1 cup of juice and pulp

one extra lemon for garnishing

chipped ice

Juice the lemons. Fanni did it with a glass juice reamer bowl, pushing down on each half and twisting with her wrist until the juice and pulp ran out. Then she picked out the seeds with a teaspoon. She poured the juice, lemon by lemon, into her big, glass, half gallon pitcher.

Then she added water and sugar and stirred. Or you can add water and simple syrup and stir. You can make simple syrup by cooking the sugar ahead of time in a cup of water. That way you get no sugar grains at the bottom of the pitcher. But isn't that part of the fun?

Chip some ice off a big block with an ice pick. Or buzz some cubes in your food processor. Add that to the lemonade.

Cut that extra whole lemon into slices and toss half of them into the lemonade pitcher. Use the other half for garnishing the glasses you drink the lemonade out of.

My Honey Lemonade

Substitute ½ to 2/3 cup of raw honey for the sugar, depending on how tart you like it

You can dissolve the honey in a cup of warm water first, before adding it to the rest. You can also buzz up the entire mixture in a blender or food processor, along with some ice.

My Juicer Honey Lemonade

Cut *organic* lemons into pieces. Pick out the seeds. Put through a veggie juicer. That way, you get some of the oils in the skin and some of the white under the skin, too. Scoop out some of the pulp and put in a food processor or blender. Add the juice and a cup of water and buzz. Add the honey and buzz. Alternatively, you can whiz chopped whole lemons and skip the veggie juicer. Pour into a pitcher and add the rest of the water and stir.

My Rosewater Lemonade

To any of the above recipes, add a tablespoon or two of rose water, which you can get at an Arab grocery store or a coop or natural food store. Gives it a nice garden flavor.

Margaret and Mom by the summerhouse

Fanni with friends in front of her milk store in Vienna

Chapter 7

Life in Vienna

Fanni's Life in Vienna

I always keep Fanni's birthday, August 2nd, as a special day to remember her by. She was the seventh in a family of eight children, delivered at home by a midwife, in 1886. Fanni's family lived in Sitzgras, 100 miles from Vienna, by rail.

Fanni's father, Mathias Schmidt, is listed on her birth certificate as a *maurer*, which is a man who makes walls, like a plasterer or bricklayer. Her mother, Johanna Wallisch, was also the daughter of a *maurer*, so maybe Johanna she met Mathias through her father. During the winter season, according to Mom, Mathias went to the towns and villages to find work.

That's because Mathias had another occupation, as a *hausler*, according to Fanni's birth certificate. Mom and I were looking at that one day and wondered what a *hausler* did. We looked in the German dictionary, but we couldn't find the word. So Mom wrote a letter to Rosa Kraus over in Vienna, asking her. Rosa had been Mom's sister Margaret's best friend in Vienna and also became Mom's friend.

Rosa's reply contained her own wonderful description of what *hauslers* did, which Mom and I translated.

> *Hauslers* lived simply in a small house, owned their own land, which they used not only to grow a vegetable garden and potato field for the family, but also a little extra to sell and buy sugar and flour and other necessaries they didn't grow themselves. They kept chickens, a pig and a goat from which they got eggs, meat and milk for their daily needs.

Fanni with her parents and a sister and brother on the family farm

Fanni's sampler that she made in school

So a *hausler* was busy with gardens in the summer and harvesting in the fall. His family, too. In the winter, when Fanni's father was away working on a building site, Johanna, ran the farm, along with Fanni and the other kids.

I asked Fanni about the farm she grew up on, one day when I was twelve years old. She came out to our house in the suburbs every week, to spend the day with us. "Ve had had goats und chickens. My chob was da goose girl – I took da geese out into the countryside every day." That way the geese could eat a good diet, without the family spending money on their feed. In her house on 20th Street, Fanni had a picture hanging up on her dining room wall, of a little goose girl leading her flock over a wooded hillside, so I think she must have enjoyed doing that. A chob she shared with her brothers and sisters, was hauling water up from the creek every day for household use. Hard work in the summer and chilly in the winter!

When Fanni was old enough to go to school, she learned sewing, in addition to the usual subjects of reading, writing and arithmetic. I have her white-on-white hand stitching sampler from school. It shows her mastery of shirring, tucking, buttonholing, button covering, patching, reweaving, embroidery, monogramming, eyelet-making, hemming and placarding. These were all skills a girl was likely to use working for her family or for an employer.

Fanni only went to school through the 8th grade, but back then the standards were a lot higher. Fanni was good at arithmetic, because she managed the family finances throughout most of her marriage. And for quite a few decades, she was Treasurer of the Wiener Blut, an Austrian social club in Milwaukee. She read both German and English, because she clipped recipes from newspapers published in both languages, when she lived in Milwaukee.

When Fanni finished school in 1899, her father took her on the train to Vienna, where he had arranged for her to work keeping house for a family. "There were too many mouths to feed on the farm," Fanni told me. By the time Fanni had turned 13, most of the other children had already grown up, so there must have been grown married children living there too, with their kids. In Vienna, housemaids like Fanni worked from dawn to well after dusk, six and a half days a week, with a half day off on Sunday. In exchange for all that work, Fanni got room and board in Vienna and a small wage. But she didn't get to keep her pay. She had to send that back home to her parents.

Fanni met Johann in 1908, when she had been in Vienna going on nine years. You might wonder how a 22 year old girl, with only a half day off on Sundays, would have time to find someone she wanted to marry. She found him in her own backyard. Fanni lived and worked up on the second floor of an apartment building, and Johann boarded with another family on the first floor. He worked in Vienna as a precision assembly worker in a microscope factory, but he had grown up in the country, too, not far from Fanni's hometown, in Grosswaltersdorf, north of Vienna. Like Fanni, he had been sent to Vienna to make his way in the world.

Following a country custom, at night when work was done and it was dark, Johann set a ladder under her second story bedroom window. He climbed up and courted her through the window, like Romeo and Juliet. That same year, he gave her a gold engagement ring, set with a small ruby and two diamond chips, inscribed, *Hans 1908.*

Karlskirche in the snow

Fanni & Johann's wedding portrait

Fanni and Johann's Life Together

Two years later, when she was 24, Fanni was still two years short of the age of majority for women. Thus her father gave her a handwritten note with his permission for her to marry. On March 14, 1910, Fanni and Johann married in Vienna's beautiful, fashionable Karlskirche. Then they moved into an apartment in Vienna's Hernals, a working class neighborhood that stretched from the Gürtel to the Vienna woods. That was a part of town well suited to people like Fanni and Johann who had grown up in the country, because it featured lot of meadows, woods and parks [which are still there today]. Like many apartments in those days, they lived, ate and slept in one single, long, large room. Fanni had her kitchen in one corner. Johann had his workshop in another, where he made their furniture. "He put sawdust in the air and I had to keep it from getting into the food," Fanni told me years later, chuckling over what must have been a bone of contention between them, at the time.

Fanni had a dream of opening her own shop one day. That dream became a reality when she inherited a little money from a relative. Married women didn't control their own property back then, so the money went to her husband Johann, a fact she always emphasized when telling the story to me fifty years later. "Without ever showing me the check," she explained, "he bought me the store."

In 1912, Fanni stood downstairs in front of her store for a photo, with another lady and that lady's kids. Items she sold up on the second floor were listed on signs on either side of the entrance: milk, three different kinds of cream, butter, eggs, fresh baked goods, whole grain bread and candy. Her name, Fanni Baier is on the sign in the lower right. The signs are new, because the stone of the building is chipped, where the iron of the sign with the cow meets the wall.

It's a warm day in spring. The window is open on the second floor. Fanni wears a bib apron over a skirt made of a heavy fabric and a ¾ sleeve blouse, suitable for a working woman. Her friend holds an umbrella in hand, ready for a spring shower, her baby is dressed in several layers, and her half grown daughter wears a cape, suggesting that they were out for a walk, perhaps to do their early morning marketing before the daughter went to school.

Above the entrance, hangs a sign for Ankerbrot, a popular Viennese brand of hearty bread. Fanni had it for sale upstairs, because as the sign says, she was a *verkaufstelle*, or an official outlet. Back when the picture was taken in 1912, Ankerbrot was a large bakery, with 25 bakers and 1300 employees, supplying bread and rolls all over the city of Vienna. The anchor is a contemporary symbol of security and trust. Next to the anchor you see the Hapsburg seal, a double-headed eagle, wearing a crown and wielding a sword, indicating that Anchorbrot supplied the royal household of the Hapsburgs. The prestige this appointment lent helped Anchorbrot outstrip its competitors. The brand survives to the present day, specializing in hearty, whole grain breads that make your average loaf of American whole wheat bread seem wimpy.

All in all, Fanni's milk store was quite a success story for a girl, who grew up herding geese in the country, and went to seek her fortune in the capital city of a great empire.

Johann's passport photo

On Sundays, Fanni made up a picnic lunch and went with Johann up into the mountains ringing Vienna on three sides, with a hiking club called the "Oderquelle." The group traipsed the high trails that wound around the city, singing songs as they went. At midday, everyone lolled on the grass, munched their picnic lunches and read the newspaper.

Fanni and Johann also enjoyed walking to outdoor wine gardens in outlying districts of Vienna, located several miles from their home, in Grinzing and Nussdorf. In those days, they brought their own cold chicken in a picnic basket and purchased a bottle of wine from the vintner when they arrived at a *Heurigen* wine garden. They got a table and relaxed and enjoyed *gemulichkeit,* sipping wine, singing songs and dancing to *Shrammelmusik,* played by musicians on violin, bass and accordion. The sentimental songs told of feeling homesick, or honoring your wife because she puts up with you, or missing your children when they go away. *Wiestadt der Liebe,* Vienna, City of Love, is about how beautiful Vienna is. One of Fanni's favorite songs, *Der Mai Ist Gecommen,* May is A-Coming, celebrates the glory of spring, when the trees leaf out, flowers blossom and you feel your heart lift.

Lingering is part of the *Heurigen* experience. So when the chicken in the picnic basket and the wine are gone, no one feels like going home right away. So Fanni and Johann stayed, nibbling from the bag of *krammel* [cracklings] they brought with them, and singing more songs with the musicians. Then the music stops and the musicians pack up. But still, no one wants to go home just yet and bring an end such a good time.

Mom went hunting for a good *Heurigen* with Johnny, Betty and Rosa, her Austrian friend, who dressed for the occasion in a *tracht,* a traditional Austrian women's costume.

15. Wanderschaft.

1. Der Mai ist ge = kom = men, die Bäu = me schlagen aus, da
2. Frisch auf drum, frisch auf drum im hel = len Sonnenstrahl, wohl
3. O Wan = dern, o Wandern, du frei = e Burschenlust! Da

1. blei = be, wer Lust hat, mit Sor = gen zu Haus. Wie die
2. ü = ber die Ber = ge, wohl durch das tie = fe Tal! Die
3. wehtGot = tes O = dem so frisch in die Brust; da

1. Wolken dort wan = dern am himm = li = schen Zelt, so
2. Quellen er = klin = gen, die Bäume rau = schen all; mein
3. sin = get und jauch = zet das Herz zum Him = mels = zelt: wie

1. steht auch mir der Sinn in die wei = te, wei = te Welt.
2. Herz ist wie 'ne Ler = che und stim = met ein mit Schall.
3. bist du doch so schön, o du wei = te, wei = te Welt!

1854. Emanuel Geibel, 1815—1884.

16. Bescheidenheit siegt.

1. Die Ler = che singt, der Kuk = kuk schreit, Krieg
2. Die Blu = men strei = ten hef = tig = lich, wer
3. Und auch die Vö = gel strei = ten sich um
4. Da mi = schet sich der Früh = ling drein: „Was",
5. So laßt uns wie die Ro = se sein und

Der Mai Ist Gecommen from Johann's Oderquelle songbook.

One of Fanni's favorites

"We walked up these small streets, in Grinzing, a quaint, old village in the wine-growing district of Vienna," Mom wrote in her travel diary. "It was fall and the new wine was ready at little *Heurigens*, where they make their own wine. New wine has a light, fruity taste that goes down easy. If you see a branch over the door, you can go in that house and sample a glass. If it's a nice evening, they have a place outside where you can sit."

Mom's party of four wanted to make sure they didn't land in a noisy *Heurigen*, in the midst of entertaining a tour bus, so Rosa invented the ruse "that we were 'looking for Herr Maier,'" Mom writes. That way they could knock on doors and peek inside, until they found one they liked.

Most places were crowded and noisy with big tourist buses nearby. Some were elegant and ritzy. But, finally, we settled on a quiet, pretty, uncrowded little *Heurigen*, where Rosa made sure we were seated at the musician's table. He was an older gentleman with a guitar playing folk songs, and Rosa knew how to butter him up, with compliments and tips, so he obligingly played all our requests.

Rosa ordered wine and chicken for us and we sat back for hours, eating and drinking and listening to the guitarist's wonderful repertoire of old Viennese songs, which Rosa and he sang so beautifully. I especially enjoyed one about a little bird who lost his love and had a lot of hard luck. But he could never be sad, because he always had his little song that was music to his ears, and no one could take that away from him.

Another Viennese pastime Fanni and Johann enjoyed was going to a coffee house. "Some of the cafes are still in operation today," Mom told me, "like the Cafe Mozart or the Cafe Central, where notables used to get together in my parent's day and talk about the big questions in life." Yeah, like artists and writers, Freud and even Trotsky. In a Viennese cafe, you can still stay all day, sipping your coffee, talking with friends and reading from a large selection of magazines and papers.

Fanni and Johann always drank their coffee with cream and sugar. In Vienna, they don't do black coffee. They drink coffee with milk or with *schlag,* a heavy cream that might come whipped. Mom says, "if you order just a plain cup of coffee in Vienna, it came *"sprudelt,"* meaning it came with milk or *schlag,* aerated with a beater to produce a foamy top. That's different from a latte, for which foam is made by forcing steam though it, with an ear splitting espresso machine.

Speaking of Viennese coffee, one of my Mom's sister Margaret's favorite songs was *In Einem Kleinem Cafe in Hernals.* Hernals is the district where Margaret lived with Fanni and Johann in Vienna, until she was seven years old and they came to America. The song tells of two lovers drinking *mocca* in a plain little cafe in Hernals. A record player plays a song softly in the background. The lovers sit there gazing into each other's eyes. The cafe finally closes, unnoticed by the couple. The innkeeper turns the lights down low and quietly leaves the lovers to themselves.

Johann's brother Alois at a Conditorei in Vienna

The Oderquelle, tramping in the Vienna Woods

If you didn't come to the cafe with some you are deeply in love with, you can still enjoy something sweet. "You can pick out a nice pastry there," Mom reports, "like a *krapfen*, which is a sweet roll with a jelly filling. Or you can get a kuchen, made with a *Murbeteig* base and fruit on the top. There are strudels, made from *Strudelteig*, a very tricky recipe, filled with fruit, sour cream or dessert cheeses. Or you can have something made with *Biskuitteig*, a spongy cake, usually filled and topped with something like strawberries and heavy cream."

My cousin Renate served us up a strawberry shortcake made with *Biskuitteig*, that was a sight to behold, piled high with sour cream and ruby red strawberries! Cafes also offer tortes, like Sacher torte, which Mom points out "is sometimes made with ground nuts to substitute for flour and butter.

Another place Fanni and Johann liked to go to relax was a pastry shop, called a *Konditerei*. Mom explains, "They usually have a big window in front with a whole, wonderful, array of delicious things you can sit down and eat with your coffee. It's beautiful to see. You choose from little things that would take a couple of bites to eat, to torts, to big sweet rolls." In Vienna today, Konditerei are still popular places, where people go during an afternoon break from work.

Fanni and Johann also went to dances where they waltzed to music of Johann Strauss, like *Tales of the Vienna Woods* and *The Blue Danube*, played by a small live orchestra. Dancing, wine gardens, hiking up in the mountains, sipping a leisurely *Kaffee mit Schlag* in a cafe, eating something sweet and wonderful in a Kondeiteri, these were the idyllic times Fanni and Johann enjoyed in Vienna, early in their marriage.

During these pleasant times, Fanni gave birth to their son, Hansi, in 1911. But by the time they got to America, all they had left of their little boy was a large picture of him that hung over Grandma's bed. My mother, born to Fanni after they came to America relates, "neither one of my parents would talk about my brother. Either it was too painful for them to talk about or they thought I shouldn't know about it."

In America, they often got teary listening to their collection of 78 records of Strauss waltzes and *Shramelmusik*, remembering the lives they once lived, in the beautiful capital city of a vanished Austro-Hungarian empire.

The Great War

Hard times lay ahead, when the Great War began in 1914. Johann was drafted into the Austro-Hungarian Army. At the time he left for his military service, Fanni was pregnant with their second child, Margaret, who she gave birth to after Johann left for the military. Fanni and Johann didn't see each other again for four years. They only managed to pass a few letters to each other during the war.

I have a picture postcard Johann sent Fanni in 1916, of his military unit lined up in formation, comprised of men back home in the countryside, where he had been raised. Johann drew an arrow pointing over his head, then scrawled in pencil across the front of the card, "Greetings to everyone from the country bumpkins." He also scribbled on the postcard picture, "the magnificent heather-gatherers." He is probably poking fun at the fact that they were all country-raised boys, unaccustomed to fighting before they were drafted.

Johann's unit was stationed at the front near France and his military service was no laughing matter. And, during the four terrible years he was gone, Fanni was left on her own in Vienna, struggling to provide for her two small children in a world of harsh deprivation, not knowing if she would ever see Johann again.

She had already lost the milk store before the war began. In the day when husbands by law controlled their wives' money, Johann mortgaged Fanni's store. He didn't tell her what he had done. He just took the money and gave it to a friend who needed it for a business deal, a friend who, according to Mom, "he would walk through flames for." Fanni, who knew nothing of the deal, continued waiting on customers as usual, selling milk, bread, butter, eggs, sweet rolls and candy. But when Johann's friend's business venture turned sour, Fanni learned of the business deal between them which involved a mortgage on her property. And that's how she lost the store.

With the men gone to the front, Vienna had become a city of women and children. Starving women and children. Before the war, food and fuel had been plentifully supplied to Vienna from the vast resources of the Austro-Hungarian Empire. However, when those lines of supply dried up during the war, food and fuel were extremely hard to come by in the city. Fanni told me, "I had to stand all day in long lines for hours, in all kinds of weather, just to get a crust of bread or a lump of coal." She waited her turn with her baby Margaret in her arms and her little son Hansi at her side.

It must have been very difficult for a woman who had recently owned a milk store to not only lose her dream, but to find herself standing line for food and coal. But was not in Fanni's nature to hold a grudge. Later, in America, however, Fanni took charge of their finances. Johann had to sign his pay check over to her as soon as he got home with it.

"Greetings to all from the Country Bumpkins"

"The Idyllic Heather Gatherers"

Johann, foreground, spotter in a machine gun trio

Johann served his country as a scout, advancing ahead of the artillery, drawing fire, so leaders could assess the strength of the enemy and decide where to aim their big guns. He was part of a machine gun team of three men. One guy operated the gun mounted on a tripod, while another fed the belt of ammunition into the gun. Johann was the spotter, scanning for the enemy with a pair of Zeiss binoculars. He was likely assigned to that duty because of his work as a precision assembler in the microscope factory, because he would have known how to maintain his binoculars in the field. His job was to alert the other two, when he spotted the enemy lying in ambush, and help them direct their fire so they hit their target. When I was a teenager, I used to put his Zeiss binoculars up to my eyes and wonder, like I was in a Twilight Zone episode, if I could see what he had seen during the war. Good thing that didn't work, because, according to Mom, Johann had seen "unspeakable things."

In Vienna, Fanni was coping on her own, with their two children. But it was hard without enough food coming into the capital city. Margaret, who was a toddler, developed rickets, a nutritional deficiency, in which the bones grow weak and become curved. Eventually she recovered, but not until after the war was over. A year after the war started, four-year old Hansi developed a high fever. As Fanni told it to Mom, "All the available doctors were sent to the front lines to aid the wounded, so there was no medical help for the citizens left behind." Hansi died. She had gotten word to Johann, because when Fanni got that postcard from him, he addressed it to her and Gretel [Margaret's nickname]. He also mentioned that Fanni's idea to visit him would have been a hardship for her. He might have been referring to the expense of the trip, or he could have been considering the burden another wartime pregnancy would have had on her.

At Fanni's house, I used to see her make the sign of the cross on the bottom of a new loaf of bread. She explained to me she did that as "a prayer of thanks for having it." Other times she sighed and looked down, her eyes heavy with sadness that she never verbalized. But there was one time I'll never forget, when I was licking my wounds over a boyfriend, and she said to me, "Sometimes it hurts to love." Wow. It was like an arrow had shot straight from her heart to mine.

When Johann came home from the war, he was a changed man. He had a wounded leg. He also suffered from "shell shock" and had developed severe asthma, from being exposed to mustard gas. The leg wound healed, although my mother says he always limped when people weren't looking. But shell shock and asthma wrought havoc on him for the rest of his life. Mustard gas is a purely evil invention, a chemical weapon, with a corrosive effect that takes 24 hours to develop. That way people don't necessarily notice when they are exposed until the next day, by which time the chemical has penetrated their clothing, not only causing serious skin burns, but also searing their lungs, which can result in pulmonary edema and asthma. All three health conditions can be lethal. In Johann's case, he had asthma for the rest of his life. Many years after he was exposed, he died of cancer, one more lethal symptom of mustard gas.

When Johann returned from the war, he found Fanni living in the same apartment where he had left her four years before. He was wounded. She was thin. They had lost their son to illness. But they were together, now. She introduced him to his daughter, Margaret, who he had never seen before. By this time Gretel was four years old.

Fanni and Hansi

Chapter 8

Meat Dishes

Goulash

Codified by Mom

1 lb. Beef cut for stew

2-3 T Fat or oil

3 Onions, chopped

1 tsp. Paprika

Caraway seeds

¼ tsp. Cayenne pepper

1 tsp. Salt

2 Quartered carrots

2 Diced potatoes

1 Stalk chopped celery

Water

Fry onions in fat or oil until brown.   Add paprika and meat, browning slowly.   Add ½ cup of water and the caraway seeds, sharp pepper and salt.   Cook for at least 2 hours or until tender, stirring frequently.   Add water as necessary.

For gravy, in a separate container, add 1 T flour to a little water, making a paste.   Stir the paste into the stew.   In the last half hour of cooking, you can add quartered carrots, diced potatoes, celery, etc.

Serve in a big serving dish with the liquid.

Wienerschnitzel

Codified by Mom

Filleted meat

Salt and pepper to taste

Flour

Beaten egg

Breadcrumbs

This dish is made from either veal or chicken or turkey breast. If you can't find humanely raised veal, use beef.

Cut up thin fillet slices of veal, chicken or turkey breast. You can also use beef or venison fillets. Remove fat. Pound thin with a wooden mallet. If you don't have a mallet, you can use the flat side of a rolling pin. Salt and pepper the meat.

Prepare 2 separate wide, flat bowls [like soup bowls] of flour and beaten egg. Press pounded fillets into the bowl of flour. Then dip into the bowl of beaten egg. Lastly, lay on top of breadcrumbs, that you have sprinkled on a breadboard, and pound with your fist on both sides to press breadcrumbs into the cutlet.

Fry in a frying pan in lots of hot fat or oil, until golden brown.

Serve with lemon wedges, which are squeezed over the schnitzel at the table.

Wiener Chive Sauce

from my Viennese cousin Renate

5 semmeln rolls
a little milk
5 egg yolks
5 tablespoons of mayonnaise
salt, pepper, sugar, vinegar, water, chives

Grate rolls, soak in milk. When milk is soaked up, about 20 minutes, mix rolls and milk with mayonnaise and egg yolks.

Season with salt, pepper, sugar, vinegar, adding water as needed to make a sauce. Spoon onto Wienerschnitzel. Sprinkle chives over the top.

Healthy alternative: skip the egg yolks and mayo, substitute nayonaise or other vegan mayo.

My Cousin Renate Serving Wienerschnitzel in Vienna to her Mom, Fini, who later was called Rudi. Fini is Fanni's niece and Renate is Fanni's great niece.

Gluten-free, Veal-free Wienerschnitzel

From my friend, Carol Hirschi

Chicken breast - use natural free range for compassion and taste

Beaten egg

Almond meal

Walnut oil

Pound chicken breasts flat with mallet or rolling pin. Bread by dipping in egg, then almond meal. Pan sauté in walnut oil. Serve with lemon wedges.

Johann, Betty and Fanni

Sauerbraten or Lammfleisch

Codified by Margaret's daughter, Betty

Serve with bread dumplings and red cabbage for an authentic Austrian dinner. Betty just made this for Thanksgiving and it was really good!

Sauerbraten is a marinated beef dish. Lammfleisch is a marinated lamb dish. After sitting in vinegar in your frig for 3 days and then several hours of cooking, this meat will be very tender.

Lamb: a roast or

Beef: Top round roast is best. You can also use the bottom round or rump. The main thing is it should be a lean chunk of meat

Vinegar

Water

Sliced onion

2 Heaping tsp. pickling spice

Lard or oil

Sliced carrots

Sliced celery

Add salt and pepper if desired [there may already be some in the pickling spice]

Flour and water for gravy

Put meat in a Dutch oven or roasting pan with a cover.

In a 3 qt. saucepan, combine 2 parts water to 1 part vinegar. You can try 2 cups water to 1 cup vinegar. There should be enough liquid to cover the meat.

Add one sliced onion and 2 heaping teaspoons of pickling spice. Heat to steaming. Pour over meat. Cool down and then refrigerate for three days, turning the meat at least once a day.

When you are ready to cook, pat the meat dry, removing all the spices. Put the brine through a sieve, but save the sliced onions to cook with the meat. Brown the meat well on all sides in lard or oil. Add a little water or brine to rinse brown bits from the side of the pan. Add reserved onion, sliced carrots and celery. Cover meat with equal parts water and brine, keeping about 1 ½ inches of liquid in the bottom of the pan at all times. Simmer about 2 hours until tender.

Remove the meat and slice. Make a flour and water paste in a cup and add to the liquid in the pan to make gravy. Cook a few minutes. Strain the gravy and pour over the meat in a large serving bowl.

Stew

Codified by Mom

This stew was originally made with veal. If you cannot obtain some humanely raised veal, please substitute with beef, buffalo, venison or other red game.

Cubed stew meat

Chopped onion

Paprika

Salt

Flour

Water

Brown chopped onion and cubed meat. Add quite a lot of paprika and some salt. Cook in a small amount of water until done, about an hour. Thicken gravy with a paste of flour and water made in a cup, then add to the juices and simmer briefly.

Personally, I like to make stew with red wine and rosemary. If I have no red wine, then I used balsamic vinegar or if I have no balsamic, then just white or apple cider vinegar. They all help tenderize the meat and give the dish a tangy flavor. I cook for an hour and a half to two hours for really tender meat.

Meat Balls

Codified by Mom, maybe

I think this may have come off of a canned soup label.   But Fanni used to make it in America and I grew up on it at Mom's. In fact, it was my favorite dinner dish at home, except for the batter fried Lake Michigan perch we got from the deli on Fridays.

1 lb. ground beef

1 medium onion, chopped

salt and pepper to taste

1 egg

bread crumbs or bread slices soaked in water

1 can of tomato soup

green pepper (optional)

celery (optional)

Combine all ingredients, except soup, celery and green pepper, and shape into balls.   Combine 1 can of tomato soup with ½ can water, and stir.   Heat until simmering. Add meat balls.   Green pepper chunks, celery or celery leaves added to the soup gives added flavor.   Cook covered for ½ hour.

Serve in a big serving bowl.

Rouladen
Pigs in a Blanket

Reconstructed by Mom

Round steak

Chopped onion

Bacon

String or toothpicks

3 T Fat or oil

Water

Flour

Cut up pieces of very thin round steak, trimming off fat. Pound flat with a wooden mallet. Chop onion and bacon and lay some on each piece of meat. Roll up and tie with string or fasten with a toothpick. Brown on all sides in hot fat or oil. Add a small amount of water and simmer about 1 hour until tender. Put some water and meat juices in a cup and puree to make a paste with flour and add to remaining liquid. Heat to make gravy. Serve gravy in a boat.

Round Steak

Codified by Mom

slice of beef round steak, ½ inch thick

1/6 cup of butter

1/6 cup of oil

1 medium onion, sliced in rings

salt and pepper to taste

1 tsp. paprika

a little cayenne

water

Salt and pepper a slice of round steak. Brown in half butter and half oil (about 1/3 cup combined). Add 1 medium onion, chopped and 1 tsp. of paprika, and brown some more. Add a small amount of water, cover and cook until tender, about 1 ½ hours. Add more water as necessary and turn the meat occasionally.

When tender, remove from the pan, trim fat and cut into serving sized pieces. Mix some flour and water into a smooth slurry and add to the pan. Cook up the gravy and strain. Put meat and gravy into a big serving dish.

Baked Whole Chicken

Reconstructed by Mom

A whole chicken - use a free range, natural chicken

Lard or butter

Salt

Water

Flour for gravy

     Grease a whole chicken (free range natural) with lard or butter (or, my health variation, olive oil and rub with a crushed clove of garlic).   Rub with salt.

     Bake at 350 degrees for 45 minutes in a covered pan with a little water in the bottom.   Raise the temperature to 400 for the last half hour, or more, till done.   In this phase, leave the bird uncovered and baste with juices in the pan frequently, for a nice, crispy skin.

     Make gravy by removing the chicken from the pan. Take some juices and mix with flour to make a paste in a cup. Gradually add some more juices.   Then add to the rest of the juice and stir.   Strain if you like. Serve in a gravy boat.

Bread Dumplings

Codified by Mom

Serve these with a nice meat dish, like Sauerbraten, Goulash, Stew or Roulaten. Cover with gravy. Left over dumplings can be cut into slices and fried in butter. That way they are almost better than they were the first time.

3 stale Kaiser rolls or 6 pieces of stale bread, cubed

1 egg, beaten plus enough milk to make ½ cup liquid

3 T flour to ½ cup

salt

pepper

Start by soaking stale Kaiser rolls or bread about 2 hours ahead of cooking time. The bread or rolls should be very hard. Allow at least two slices of bread or one hard roll per dumpling. Cut into chunks about the size of a bread cube or shave the rolls with a paring knife.

Mix a slightly beaten egg with a little milk to make about half a cup of liquid. Add salt and pepper. Pour over rolls and let sit about half an hour to soak in. Then push and work the dough with your fingers every so often, adding a little water as needed, over the next hour and a half. All the cubes should be moistened, or the dumplings will turn out hard. The dough should be soft, but not so mushy you can squeeze out liquid.

Sprinkle 3 T to a half a cup of flour over the dough and work it in. The dough should now form a large ball, with all the bread moistened. Do not make too wet or they will fall apart. Too dry and the dumplings will be hard

.

Wet hands and form into balls about 2" in diameter. Put them in enough boiling salted water that they will be completely covered. Boil about 10 minutes, stirring occasionally so that they do not stick to the bottom of the pan. Remove with a slotted spoon.

It's a good idea, until you become experienced at it, to start by boiling a test dumpling first, to make sure your dough is going to hold together and make nice, firm dumplings. If it falls apart, add more flour and try another test dumpling.

Makes 6 dumplings

.

For 15 Dumplings:

20 slices of bread

4 eggs and milk to make 2 cups of liquid

¾ cup flour

For 20 Dumplings:

1 lb. loaf of stale bread

5 eggs and milk to make 2 ½ cups of liquid

1 cup flour

Wiener Semmelknoedel - Dumplings

Codified by Mom

5 stale rolls

1 stick butter [4 oz]

½ to 1 cup milk

2 eggs

¼ cup flour

1 small onion, finely chopped

1 tsp parsley, chopped

pinch of salt

Dice rolls and toast lightly in oven. Saute onion in butter until glossy. Add parsley. Pour over cubes and mix well. Whisk milk, eggs and salt, and pour over mixture. Let rest for about an hour to soak up the liquid. Mix again and add flour. With wet hands, form large dumplings. Put in a pot of boiling, salted water and let simmer 10 minutes, making sure the dumplings don't stick to the bottom of the pan. When they rise to the top they are done.

Tafelspitz – Boiled Beef Fillet

From Renate in Vienna

Tafelspitz is often called, the "national dish of Austria." I don't remember having it at Grandma's. But we did have this in Vienna at a restaurant with my Austrian Tante Rudi, Fanni's niece. Also in the dinner party were Rudi's daughter, Renate, her grandson Bernhard and his wife Elke, along with Tante Rudi's other daughter Ingrid and her husband Gunter. I brought little gifts for everyone and I remember I gave Gunther a little framed life drawing I had done of a nude woman. He liked that a lot!

This recipe comes from Renate. You can use American or Austrian measurements for your ingredients.

5 lb. [2.5 kg] rump roast

¼ lb [100 g] beef bones
¼ lb [100 g] beef liver
¼ lb [100 g] of bovine spleen [oops, no spleen? Try doubling the liver]
3 cloves of garlic [don't think Fanni ever cooked with garlic]
2/3 lb. [300 g] of roots, such as carrots, yellow turnips, celery, or leeks
1 good sized [100 gms] onion
salt

pepper

chives

2 bay leaves

Blanche the bones [cook the bones briefly] in boiling water. Rinse them in hot, then cold water. Put the blanched bones, with liver and spleen in cold water on the stove. Bring to a boil, skim off the foam repeatedly until it no longer forms.

Now add the boiled beef with garlic, bay leaf and peppercorns and let the pot simmer slowly for 1 hour. Meanwhile, cut the onion in half with the peel on and sauté it in a pan. Add the browned onion and raw root vegetables to the pot and let boil for another hour.

Then remove the meat and keep warm.

Here various recipes diverge on how it is served at table, so I will tell you how we ate it in Vienna. A large tureen came from the restaurant's kitchen to our outdoor table in the enclosed garden. We ladled it into our soup bowls ourselves. It had the root vegetables in it, but you can strain them out if you like a clear broth. Then, when we were done with the soup, a platter of meat came to the table, the same meat that had been boiled in the soup. It had been kept warm and moist in the kitchen and sliced just before serving. We helped ourselves to as much meat as we wanted on our dinner plates.

Typically, the meat is served with fried potatoes and a horseradish sauce, with perhaps a few chives sprinkled over the meat.

Renate suggests sprinkling the meat with coarse salt when serving. Her recipe for a horseradish condiment to serve with Tafelspitz is next.

Semmelkren

A traditional condiment for Tafelspitz

From Renate in Vienna

3 sliced semmeln rolls
¼ cup butter
1 ½ cups soup
salt and pepper
sugar
1 T grated horseradish

Cut rolls into slices and fry in butter. Pour in beef broth and cook for 2 minutes. Season with salt, pepper and a little sugar. Season with grated horseradish.

Reisfleisch

A dish to make with leftovers

Cut up goulash or stew leftovers into small pieces, about ½ " in size. Place meat in a buttered or oiled skillet, along with gravy and cooked rice. Heat, stirring to coat rice.

Bacon Drippings

The drippings from cooking bacon were poured, while still liquid, into a pre-cycled can, such as vegetables come in. Johann liked to use this as a spread on his rye bread. Herman did, too. It looked awful to me, as a child. It's flavorful, but high in cholesterol, so I don't recommend using this today.

Krammeln

These are cracklings, bits of meat made crispy in the process of rendering lard. Eat with a spoon for a snack. That's what Fanni and Johann brought from home and nibbled on at the *Heurigens*.

Mom writes:

> "In the older days, Viennese women rendered their own lard from fat purchased at the butcher. Using huge kettles, they would melt and simmer the fat until crunchy bits rose to the top. It looked like granola. Krammeln were crisp and made a tasty snack.
>
> After skimming, the fat then was rendered into white lard. Not done anymore, because you need massive pots and who sells big chunks of fat anymore?"

A modern, healthy, yummy alternative is to chop garlic fine and pan sauté in extra virgin olive oil. No cholesterol! Sprinkle a little salt on it and eat it with a spoon.

Fanni and Johann's passports

Chapter 9

A New Dream

By the close of the Great War, the great Austro-Hungarian Empire of 50 million people was gone, broken apart into a number of countries.   Vienna, once the hub of the huge empire, was now just the capitol of a small country: Austria. Day to day living conditions in the city were extremely difficult during and after the war, with food shortages, lack of work, astronomically high taxes and spiraling inflation. Fanni and Johann somehow survived the next three years, thankful to be back together again.

One day a lifeline came in the mail from America, an invitation from Johann's brother, Alois. Alois had emigrated in 1912, right before the Great War, to join an Austrian friend, Oscar Adam.   In this letter, Alois offered to sponsor Johann, Fanni and Margaret.   They could live temporarily in his household up in northern Wisconsin, and Johann could work in the small bakery that Alois ran.

Fanni and Johann grabbed at the opportunity to get back on their feet.   They fully intended to return to Vienna one day, when things there got better.   I still have the huge inventory of furniture and household items they left in storage with friends in Vienna.   Into an extra-large steamer trunk, Fanni packed their clothes and the minimum stuff they would need.   Johann brought along his German song books of tunes he sang with the Oderquelle, but Mom says she never heard him sing in America.

Fanni was 35 years old, Johann 43, and Margaret seven, when they sailed in 1921 on steerage tickets, which my Mom thinks were probably purchased by Alois as a loan.   The food for steerage passengers was so bad it was nearly inedible. Dormitory bunks were crowded together in airless rooms below decks, where seasick passengers vomited onto the unwashed floor. A complete lack of privacy and filthy toilet

The misery of steerage written on their faces -

Johann left with pipe, Fanni back row right, Gretel on her left

The ship navigating icy waters

rooms made bathing impossible on the 12 day trip. Women were constantly sexually harassed and assaulted by crew members and passengers. The steerage deck, with its smoke stacks raining cinders, was the only place to get air. You can see the miserable conditions of steerage written on their faces.

Like all immigrants, they arrived in America at Ellis Island. There Johann was detained, because during the routine medical inspection, it was discovered he had an infection in his finger. Fanni and Margaret were housed separately from Johann, in the women's quarters at Ellis Island. They had to stay there ten days, until Johann's finger healed. Finally he was released and they traveled to their final destination - Phillips, way up by Lake Superior in the northern part of Wisconsin.

Working in his brother Alois's bakery was difficult for Johann, because the dust from the flour aggravated his asthma. To further complicate matters, the two brothers were at loggerheads over the way Alois treated his wife, Kathi (pronounced Katy). She was an educated woman, who Alois had fetched and brought to America, when he was on a wife-finding mission in Austria some years before. But she didn't know that bakers are notoriously ill tempered. Their bad personalities come from having to get up everyday before dawn, and then trying to sleep during the day, when everyone else is up and making noise. So they are cranky from lack of sleep and miss a lot of family socializing.

After Alois married Kathi, according to Mom,

> He made her life miserable. She was always complaining about how cruel he was to her. He was not treating her like a human being. She had the house and then three kids to take care of and meals to cook and she had to open

the store at 6 am.   And if she didn't do that there'd be hell to pay.   It was a demanding life. She became just a shell of what she had been.

Mom says, "My father didn't like that.   He respected women and he respected Fanni.   Then, when he saw Alois hit Kathi, he stood up to him and he got kicked out."

Milwaukee

Fanni, Johann and Margaret had just come to America, gotten settled, and now they had to move again.   They couldn't go back to Vienna.   They had very little money. They didn't speak English.   So the three of them went to try their luck in Milwaukee, the largest city in Wisconsin, two hours north of Chicago.   In 1921, it was the ideal American city for Austrian immigrants.   It had a large German-speaking population, plenty of German and Austrian social clubs and over 20 German language newspapers.   Milwaukee even had a tradition of German-speaking mayors.   In addition, Milwaukee was an industrial city, where there were plenty of work opportunities for Johann.

Down in Milwaukee, they got serious about rebuilding their lives.   They rented a house on 12th and Kilbourn, in the heart of the German-speaking neighborhood, just west of downtown.   Fanni found work nearby, cleaning houses. Johann got a job a few blocks from their house, at the Hahn Bakery on 16th and Juneau.   Even though his asthma was still a problem, he kept it up, because it was the only trade he had that he could practice in Milwaukee.   In Vienna, he had been a precision assembler in a microscope factory, but there were no jobs requiring that level of skill in Milwaukee. When seven-year old Margaret was enrolled in school she didn't speak much English and had to tough it out. Fanni and Johann took English lessons. Eventually, they both spoke English well, but Johann never spoke it at home, because he wanted to keep his family in form, so they would remember their mother tongue when they returned to Vienna.

Milwaukee proved to be a haven for Fanni and Johann, where they not only found work and housing, but also conversed in their native language, danced to the Viennese music they loved, and took part in a community of people they shared the same cultural traditions with. They became members of the Wiener Blut (Vienna Blood) Club, where Johann served as president, and Fanni served as treasurer, for decades. Fanni and Johann walked to the club's dances, with a live orchestra, at Jefferson Hall on 27th and Fond du Lac. They also went to dances held by other German speaking groups, that took place every Saturday night in the German neighborhood.

One day in the mid 1920's, the house they rented on 12th and Kilbourn burned down. Fortunately, they had saved up enough money to finance a house on 16th Street. It was a small house, which they heated with a big wood-burning cook stove. It had electricity, but no plumbing or running water. They had to draw their water with a pump in the kitchen, and heat it up for washing and bathing. Like many houses in Milwaukee, it had a "Polish basement," a flat, half below ground level, with tall windows. Fanni and Johann rented that out to a nice family, the Walters. Johann built the octagon-shaped summer house there, out of scrap lumber that he scrounged out in the street.

Mom and Margaret on 16ᵗʰ Street

Three years after Fanni and Johann came to America, my Mom was born in 1924. "I had to call my Dad, '*Vater*,'" Mom remembers.

> I always had to address him in German. Otherwise he would ignore me. It was very annoying, especially when I was a teenager and I told him so. 'You're in America now. You should talk to me in American!' He did that for a purpose, so I would learn German.

Many years later, when Mom taught me Austrian German, she said, "The German you learned from me, that came from him."

Walking

Mom remembers that her family walked everywhere. It was their mode of transportation. On really hot nights, the whole family walked four miles to Bradford Beach, where they slept out in the open, with other families. There they enjoyed the cool shore breeze and slept on blankets to the sound of the waves of Lake Michigan. In case you haven't been to Milwaukee, Lake Michigan acts as a big refrigerator in the summer. Cold air from the lake hovers about 1/2 of a mile inland, and on a hot day, when you are walking down the street, you can feel the change in temperature, when you walk through a wall of cold air. You could never sleep on the beach now – you'd be hauled off by the police for vagrancy.

On Sundays, the family walked two miles to Washington Park or five miles to Lake Park. There they listened to a live concert of band music and picnicked on the grass.   Fanni packed a basket of cold Wienerchnitzel and potato salad – not the mayonnaise type but the kind made with vinegar, onions and crumbled bacon.   The City of Milwaukee was laid out so that no one would live more than a mile from a city park, which was considered to be a convenient walking distance in those days.   It wasn't just Fanni's family.   Everybody walked back then, at all hours of the day and night, and didn't think twice about it.

When Mom was a teenager, she used to walk the four miles down to the beach regularly.   She says, "If you wanted to go to the beach, you had to walk."   She even walked out to Hales Corners to go horseback riding, a distance of 10 miles each way.

20th Street

In 1929, the family moved to a bigger property at 1024 N. 20th Street.   Fanni and Johann had been stashing money away for a down payment for quite a few years.   Now they made a big step up to a house with running water, sinks and bathrooms.   They brought the summer house with them, too, on a flat bed truck.

I remember my Dad saying that Johann thought the land might have commercial potential, because it was three houses from the corner, and maybe one day a gas station would buy the property and Johann could make some money reselling it.   That never materialized, but they did have an income from the property, renting out the apartment upstairs.

Johann still worked in the bakery, but his asthma grew steadily worse.   Finally, according to Mom, he was so sick that Fanni wrote to Alois, Johann's brother, who he had had no contact with, since Alois had kicked them out of Phillips ten years before. Fanni wrote, "You should come down to Milwaukee and see him. He's your brother, you should be with him. He's going to die of very bad asthma." Alois came to see him and the two brothers reconciled. And Johann didn't die, afterall.

Alois and his Family

Thus, Mom began spending her summers with Alois and Kathi and their three kids. Alois's family had moved down from up north and opened up a bakery in Baraboo, about 40 miles northwest of the state capital in Madison. Mom became best friends with their daughter Mutz, short for Maria Antoinette, the famous daughter of 18th century Hapsburg Empress, Maria Theresa, who grew up to become the Queen of France. Unlike her regal namesake, Mutz was fun and goofy. Mom and Mutz were hilarious when they got together, sounding like two giggling little girls, even when they were in their 80's.

During her summers up there in Baraboo, Mom had a chance to observe the family first-hand.

> Alois was surly. He would come upstairs after baking, and sit at the kitchen table and drink.

> On Sundays, he put up a big front about being a big shot. We'd all drive around in his car. He'd parade all of us – me, my parents and sister, his two sons, his daughter Mutz and Kathi - so people could see what a great family he had. He

Mutz and my Mom, best buddies

     s

was a big fake.   One time when I was there, he hit Mutz.   I saw for myself what he did to their two boys.   They had to get up at 3 am to bake the bread when they were kids.   If they didn't, they would get a bop on the head.

When those two boys grew up they moved to Alaska, which is about as far away from Wisconsin as you can get and still be in America.

I loved going to Baraboo.   It's a cute little town, with a magical lake a few miles away.   The two giggle girls used to walk several miles from town to go to the beach.   Margaret and Johnny had a summer cottage up there for years, until the state canceled the leases and razed the cottages in the 60's.

The lake became my heaven, too: a pristine wilderness, surrounded by pine and rock covered bluffs with steep hiking trails.   One year when I was on vacation up at the lake, I stayed for about 10 years, renting a house nearby, in a wildlife refuge on another lake.   During that time, I met a childhood friend of Mutz's, named Clare, an octagenarian who drove into the driveway of my wilderness house one day with her girlfriend, and got stuck in the snow.   Clare told me a story about one time when she was a kid over at Mutz's, and came upon Kathi crying bitterly.   Apparently, Alois had just thrown their little dog out the second story window, to its death.   When I told Mom that story she said, "That sounds like something he would do."   After a while, Kathi and Alois couldn't even talk to each other. They lived together in stony silence for twenty years until Kathi died.

As a witness to all that abuse, Mutz was so afraid of men she could only appreciate them from afar, like Humphrey Bogart, whose local fan club she ran.   She spent much of her

Two brothers, reconciled, and their families

Johann at the Hahn Bakery on 16th & Juneau, Milwaukee

adult life as a spinster, working as a clerk in the town courthouse. Finally some friends got the idea to invite Mutz over to dinner at their house, and at the same time they invited a bachelor college professor, who taught at Oshkosh. Of course neither one of them knew they were being set up. When I went to their wedding in 1962, I was a half grown kid, who thought that 40 years of age, which is how old Mutz was when she got married, was a ghastly age for a bride. Even if she was still spunky and full of laughs. Of course, at the time, I had no notion that I myself would wind up unmarried, my whole life!

I met Uncle Alois, a year or so before he died in 1964, at Mutz's groaning board she held every year on my Mother's birthday. By that time Alois was just a small old man. He was hard of hearing and didn't say much. When he passed away, there was a bruhaha between Mutz and her older brothers, who came down from Alaska, and started an argument with her about not burying their father in the Catholic cemetery. That's where he rests today, so I guess she got her way.

Margaret

Mom's older sister Margaret was a personable and popular gal. She was also very beautiful, resembling movie star Marlene Dietrich. In the late 20's, Fanni and Johann were still planning on going back to Vienna, so Margaret didn't go to a four-year high school. Instead she enrolled in a two-year program for young women at Girls Technical High School. The program was designed so that teenage daughters could get their diploma early and go out and work. Johann wanted her there, instead of a regular high school, so they could make plans to go back, and she could finish high school in Austria. At Girl's Tech, she studied English, cooking, sewing and the violin.   But by the time Margaret graduated from her two-year program of study in 1930, the stock market had crashed and the Great Depression had arrived.   And there was no going back to Austria yet, because the country still had the same problems they had come to American to get away from.

Before Margaret married, she got a job in a chocolate candy factory.   Nearly every day Margaret brought home broken pieces, which is what probably got my Mom started on the road to being a lifelong chocolate lover.   When Margaret started dating her future husband Johnny, my Mom was sent along on dates with them. Margaret's job on the assembly line with the Sperry Candy Factory, allowed her to contribute to the family income.   Sperry was located down where all the factories were, in the Menominee Valley, starting with the Miller Brewery west of downtown and going south to the lake.   Their border Uncle Herman eventually worked down in that area, too, at Jack Winter, as a night watchman.

The Sperry Candy Company had been founded by a gal, named Ellen Sperry.   Ellen got her start in business as a girl, picking horseradish that grew wild along the railroad tracks, making it into a spread and selling it door to door.

When she grew up, Ellen and her husband opened the candy factory, which produced a popular chocolate covered salted nut roll, called the Chicken Dinner Bar. The ingredients included peanuts, milk, sugar and a chocolate coating, and *no* chicken. That was just a gimmick. The name, Chicken Dinner Bar, was just as wacky as their entire fleet of delivery trucks, which had huge chicken sculptures perched on them.   When The Sperry Candy Co. was winding down in 1959, one of

Chicken Dinner truck driving through Milwaukee

Margaret's wedding day. I still have Fanni's dress.

those chicken trucks was sold to Champion Chicken, a new restaurant located just around the corner from 81st and Lisbon, where Margaret and her husband Johnny bought their first house. Champion Chicken soon became their favorite place to eat. After I graduated from college, I used to drop in there at 4 p.m. on any old Saturday afternoon to join them for dinner, where I scrounged something vegetarian off the menu, like a salad and a piece of pie. Champion Chicken is still in business in Milwaukee, and maintains a chicken van.

The Great Depression

When the stock market crashed in America in late October 1929, things tough in America, with banks and businesses closing and people losing their jobs and property. Johann, who was still hanging on at the bakery, was laid off, because there weren't enough people with money to buy bread. But conditions were even worse in Vienna, with a succession of weak governments and 20% unemployment.

Fanni made ends meet during the Depression, in large part, with her cooking. Having experienced so much hardship previously in Vienna during and after the Great War, she "coped better than most," according to Mom. "If there was just a little, she already knew how to make do with it." Yeah, like shaving feathers and restuffing the pillow or feather bed, mending clothes, patching tears in sheets and darning holes in socks. And with her wonderful cooking.

For breakfast, she made farina or oatmeal, which they would have with sweet rolls, that Fanni got at the bakery before breakfast. At lunchtime, she would make a host of delicious meals called Mehlspeise ["flour eats"], out of flour, rice, noodles or stale bread, to which she added a little egg and milk.   These were dishes like Kaiserschmarren, Palatschinken, Noodles and Crumbs, Crepes and French Toast.   For dinner she served the beef soup she had been cooking all day on the back of the stove, with semmeln rolls, that - per Mom -"were shaped like a 'behind,'" along with rye bread spread with bacon grease instead of butter, and topped with American cheese and sliced cold cuts of meat.   Fanni also made dessert for dinner, like jello, pudding or more sweet rolls, all of which were cheap.

Fanni brought in cash, too, with the upstairs tenant, a lady who paid regular rent by doing sewing and alternations, for those who could still afford it.   Fanni also took in a boarder, Herman Signer.   His room was dark, because it was so close to the house next door you could just about reach out and touch the neighbors' window.   Though he was out of work at the time he moved in, he had some savings and was able to pay his keep.

Herman remained with the family until he passed away over 30 years later, except when Mom had his room for the year before her wedding. Fanni wanted Mom to enjoy having some privacy before she got married. Herman had to go live somewhere else for a while. When my parents were engaged, my Dad rented the room in the house next door, which was right across from Mom's room, an arm's length away. He also took his meals with Fanni, and hired her to do his washing.

Fanni really liked Dad.   But when Dad's mother warned Fanni not to let her daughter, (my Mom), marry her son, Fanni asked Mom, "What do you think she meant by that?" Exactly what she meant by that is the subject of my earlier book, *Secret Life, Secret Death.*

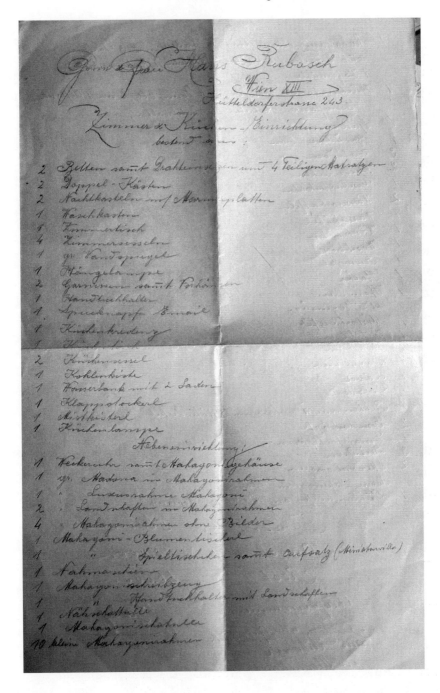

Page 1 of the inventory of things they left behind in Vienna

Another way Fanni brought in cash was walking 20 blocks to clean houses in Washington Heights, where rich people lived in big homes. She got 10 cents for several hours work, but didn't take streetcar to get there, because that cost 5 cents and would have used up her wages. So in all kinds of weather, she walked to those jobs with her little daughter Helen, my Mother, in tow. My Mom would either help her or else play quietly in a corner while Fanni worked. Fanni also worked for Dr. Hansen, who lived a couple of blocks from her house, in an apartment. She did his laundry and ironing, picking it up and delivering it. He proved to be a valuable contact for the family later on.

Mom observes, "Money was very tight. Work was hard to come by. My father would put a suit on every morning, pick up a paper and spend the rest of the day looking for work, like it was a job in itself." He also crafted furniture for their house out of odds and ends of wood. Mom says, "He used to make something out of nothing. He had a gift for carpentry work." When Fanni finally moved out of her house, she gave me a jewelry box Johann had made, with pictures on the lid and little secret drawers. It has a duplicate somewhere in Austria, with those items they left in storage.

His signature techniques were hand carved scroll work and wood inlays. He made beautiful cabinets, the dining room table, curvy end tables, magazine racks and wood framed mirrors. In addition to making his own tools, Johann made Fanni's rolling pin and Wienerschnitzel mallet. He also made a grand desk, which I have now. It's really beautiful, but I have to say, it is the most uncomfortable piece of furniture I own, because it has no leg room. Johann was a little guy. The desk fit him only when he was sitting on a special low stool he had made for it.

I found out my Grandfather's work was nearly indestructible when my brother Rob wanted a large wardrobe Johann had made shipped to him, but it was expensive to have it sent in one piece. When I dismantled the wardrobe to send it to him, I found out just how sturdy it was: Johann had even nailed the dovetail joints together! I wound up keeping the pile of dismantled wood, moving it with me from apartment to apartment, until I finally made a large mission style table for my art projects out of it. I used the doors for the top and left the key sticking in the keyhole! Johann obviously put a lot of thought into the structural engineering of each piece. His large desk doubles as my tornado shelter because I have no basement.

Johann also went out looking for repair jobs he could use his carpentry skills on, in exchange for food. It was work he could do outside, so that when he kicked up dust, it blew away in the open air, and didn't get into his lungs and bother his asthma like baking did. In the days before asthma was well understood, he smoked a pipe. They also had a dog and sometimes a cat in the house. And Herman smoked cigars. Fanni would say, "That smoke! It stinks in here!" Then she'd throw open all the windows and doors to air out the house.

Work came through Fanni and Johann's friendship with the Habenichts, who lived next door. Mom has been friends with their daughter Gretchen since childhood, which by now is over 85 years. Mr. Habenicht, had a building site ready to go in Germantown, a northwest suburb of Milwaukee. Johann offered to build them their house. The family had money to pay Johann, because their grown sons had jobs as coalmen, delivering fuel to people's houses.

Every day somebody from the Habenicht family drove Johann out to the building site in a black, square Ford sedan.   There he built them a house all by himself.

The Habenichts already had a truck patch going out there in Germantown and a batch of chickens.   They gave Johann chickens, eggs, corn and veggies to bring home.   On weekends Fanni came out with Margaret and my Mom.   That was the first time Mom ever saw a chicken running around with its head cut off.   Later, when she was a teenager, she didn't want to eat meat because she heard the cattle moaning on their way to the slaughterhouse, in trucks that whizzed by on 20th Street, on their way to pens in the Menominee Valley. She refused to eat meat if it still looked like an animal, so she only ate hamburgers and cheese sandwiches.   Mom adds, "For years I only ate American cheese on buttered Wonderbread. Yuck!"

I became a vegetarian myself for 19 years.   Then I started eating meat again, but didn't know how to tell Mom. I used to drop in on Mutz who lived in Ripon. So I asked her to break the news in one of her typed letters that she wrote to my Mom at the crack of dawn every day. Mom had been worried about me all that time and was glad to hear the news.

An elderly lady had given Fanni and Johann a $2,000 mortgage on their house, early in 1929, when they bought it. By 1933, when the Depression had been going on for four years, she wanted her $2,000 back and came to the house several times to get it. Fanni and Johann were very upset. "I want my money.   I can't live on what I have," the lady complained, along with her attorney who came with her. Mom, who was a little girl of 9 years was scared and wondered, "What's going on?"

"Luckily, FDR [Franklin Delano Roosevelt] was elected in 1932," mused Mom thinking back on those hard times. "It seemed like overnight he set up all these programs, like the FHA [Federal Housing Authority] and the WPA [Works Progress Administration] and got things going again. People were working again."

Dr. Hansen, the one Fanni did laundry for, told them about the FHA program. They saved their house by refinancing it with a government loan. Dr. Hansen also clued them in about the WPA program, where Johann found steady work. Mom says of her dad,

> He helped lay out Milwaukee's vast, beautiful Whitnall Park, a job he truly enjoyed. It was also something he could handle, because it was outdoor work and didn't bother his asthma. There were a lot of men working out there. It was a Godsend for everybody.

Johann was also hired to build a cottage out at Moose Lake, near Milwaukee. And for fun, he built replica of the first kindergarden out there for the Carl Schurz Association, a social club. Carl Schurz didn't really have anything to do with kindergartens. He distinguished himself as a journalist, Civil War general, and politician. It was his spouse, Margarethe Meyer Schurz, who taught the first kindergarten class in America in 1856, which she conducted in German, in Watertown, Wisconsin, not far from Milwaukee.

Johann also built the Wiener Blut Club floats, for German parades held on North Avenue in Milwaukee. I saw a similar parade at Germanfest in Milwaukee last summer, with folk dancers, gals in dirndls, guys in lederhosen, marching bands, Karnival royalty, and musicians in knee breeches blowing hunting horns and playing the glockenspiel.

One of Johann's floats that he built for the Wiener Blut

Mom next to word "Goethe," Margaret shortest gal on right

Fanni, Johann & Betty at the kindergarten replica

Johann built out at Moose Lake

There were Shuhplattlers in that parade, too, high-spririted, traditional, German Bavarian folk dancers, I've loved ever since I was a kid.   In time to the music, the men mime sawing wood with two-handed saws, while the women twirl.   Then the men go down on one knee and catch the hem of their partner's skirt and flip it up, revealing a flash of petticoats.   Both the women and the men yell, "EEEEEEE-YO!" when they get excited.   Next, a couple of guys get into a fist fight over a girl and pretend to slap each other.   It seems so real, because at the same time pretend to slap each other, they smack the leather lederhosen on their thighs, making a loud "whap."   When the fight is over, the ladies, who have been twirling around themselves this whole time, somehow manage to step up to the men without being dizzy, and Shuhplattling settles down, once again, into a courtship dance.

Margaret and her husband Johnny, who was German born and came to this country with his parents as a kid, used to perform Shuhplattling with a folk dancing group.   Since I was a dancer myself, I wondered how my Aunt could twirl like that for several minutes, without getting dizzy and asked her how she did it.   She replied, "Oh, it's just a trick of the foot."   That's all she would say about it.

Back in the Depression, Fanni was instrumental in getting her family through hard times.   She knew how to make a little food go a long way, with her soups and Mehlspeise.   She cleaned houses, took in laundry and ironing, collected rent from a boarder, and from the lady in the flat upstairs.   She also had a valuable contact in her employer Dr. Hanson, who not only helped them learn about the FHA loan program and keep their house, but also helped Johann with information on the WPA.

During the Depression, Fanni and Johann never had to go hungry, like those out-of-work guys who knocked at the back door, looking for food. Fanni was sympathetic and gave them a bowl of soup from the big pot she always kept on the stove, and a piece of bread. According to Mom, the men never came inside, but ate sitting on the swing in the back yard, and left when they were done eating. Mom thinks that some of them lived in the rooming houses lining their block.

Although Johann himself was often out of work due to asthma and lack of jobs, he was resourceful, too. He made his own wine and root beer, hired himself out as a carpenter for food, made handsome furniture for their home, built a house for the next door neighbors who paid him in food and cash, built a cottage out on Moose lake for money, and got that WPA job working in Whitnall Park.

Herman Signer

Their boarder Herman also contributed to the household. In addition to paying room and board, he shared the commodities he got from the county, which he was eligible for because he was not a homeowner like Fanni and Johann. Once a month he loaded up the red coaster wagon at the supply depot over the viaduct, with his ration of dry foodstuffs which he gave to Fanni.

Uncle Herman, with his gruff silence, was a permanent fixture in Fanni's dining room. When I went to her house, there he would be at the table in his undershirt, a heavy set man with light blue eyes, swathed in a swirling cloud of acrid cigar smoke, silently working on his stamp collection.

Uncle Herman at Grandpa's desk, working on stamps

Johann with the cabin he built on Moose Lake

This incomprehensibly dull, laborious process looked to me like the most boring undertaking in the world. That is, except going to school, which I had to do five days a week, plus a half day of catechism class on Saturdays.

Uncle Herman dressed and slept in a tiny side room off the dining room, separated by a lace curtain. He pulled the string to turn on the electric light during the day when he went in there, because the room was dark. The eaves of Fanni's house nearly touched those of the house next door. You could hear pigeons cooing up there when he had the window open. His tiny room had a little bed, which neatly fitted from wall to wall and hooks where he hung up his suit, trousers and hat. Next to his clothes on hangers was a dresser and stacked on top of that, a cabinet for his stamp collection. Herman's other pastime was keeping homing pigeons in the garage, which Fanni and Johann didn't need because they never own a car. He used to exchange birds with another friend who raised homing pigeons. They would release them and the birds would fly back home.

Herman had an unusual introduction to the United States, as a soldier in World War I. A German soldier. He considered himself pretty lucky to have been shot in the finger and captured during his first battle. The Americans sent him to a POW camp in New Jersey, where he says he was treated very well. Yet he must have had his share of trauma, because the story goes that his hair turned white overnight, from the shock of being shot in the little finger and taken prisoner.

When the war was over, he returned home to Germany, where he had the rotten luck to find his sweetheart had taken up with someone else, while he was a P.O.W. in America. In Milwaukee, he lived quietly with our family, and never tried romance again, in spite of the interest in an attractive, blue-eyed bachelor from ladies in the Wiener Blut.

Uncle Herman did a lot of work around our house, painting and fixing stuff. The neighbors wanted to hire him, but he would only work for us. Mom said, "He would never take a nickel for it." Uncle Herman also came out to our house on the bus and babysat for us. When he said it was time for bed, we weren't sure what would happen if we argued about it, so we just went upstairs and went to bed. Meanwhile, Uncle Herman read the paper downstairs and ate potato chips, which Fanni wouldn't let him eat at her house, because the doctor told him to keep his weight down.

When Mom was a kid, she saw a side of Uncle Herman I never did. She reports, "I used to go by him and he'd be sitting there with his stamps and he'd be all involved and I'd tickle his back as I went by or slap him playfully on top of the head and he'd laugh. I'd hold out my hand and he'd try to slap it before I pulled it away. Then he'd hold out his hand and I'd try to slap his."

Dad helped him with his paperwork. Dad also looked up to him. Apparently, Herman was the only person who could tell off my Dad. When they worked on the house together, if Herman didn't like something Dad was doing, he'd say, "That's for the shits." And Dad, who was usually a bucking bronco when it came to criticism, would take it.

Working Again

Finally in the late thirties when Mom was a young teenager, her father got a job at A.O. Smith. It was dull in comparison to his carpentry projects and the precision microscope assembly he had done in Vienna, but it paid good money. Dr. Hansen, whose washing and ironing Fanni carted back and forth to her house, was the company doctor at the factory and helped Johann get the job. During the Great War, A.O. Smith made bombs and tank frames, but by the time Grandpa worked for them, they were back to making car frames like they did before the war. Johann was able to handle working inside by this time, because medicine for asthma had recently been made available.

According to Mom, Johann always left for work dressed up in a suit, when he went to get the street car. Then, when he got to the factory, he changed into his work clothes, and then changed back to his suit to go home. When he arrived at the house, Mom says, "He had one slug of schnapps, went downstairs and did carpentry. After supper, he'd go down there and work some more. That was his relaxation," Mom recalls. "All the wood he used in his projects he either found on the street, or people gave him because they had some left over from a project. Or if something was being torn down, he would come and pick up some boards. He got a lot of it when he built that house in Germantown."

Johann had political discussions with his men friends at the house. The men closed the pocket doors and shut themselves in the front room. Mom remembers, "I heard a lot of yelling going on behind the doors." But those lively meetings at their house came to a halt after a while, because Johann didn't sympathized with the Bund and Hitler, like some of the other men did. The Bund was a pro-Nazi group of German-Americans. They had a training camp in Grafton, Wisconsin, just north of Milwaukee. "During WWII, Bund members in the U.S. were interned in camps in New Jersey, just like the Japanese," Mom said. "There were about 11,000 altogether. Some were from Milwaukee. You don't ever hear about that."

When Hitler was appointed chancellor in Germany in 1933, he established a Nazi foreign policy of absolute hegemony in Europe. Fanni and Johann decided it was best to stay put in America. In 1936, Johann became a U.S. Citizen.

World War II

In March 1938, Hitler and the Third Reich invaded Austria, uniting it with Germany in a move called the *Anschluss*. Shortly afterward, 70,000 Austrians were detained. For Fanni and Johann, returning to Vienna, even for a visit to see relatives, was out of the question. Four months after the *Anschluss*, Fanni also became a U.S. citizen in July, 1938.

During World War II nearly half of Austrian Jews, were exterminated in death camps. Austrian Christians also suffered atrocities and extreme losses at the hands of the Nazis. When the Nazis finally pulled out of Austria at the end of the war, the final insult came when the Russians invaded the country, raping women, looting, plundering, taking over residences and removing civilian men and boys. Many of these males were never heard from again, because they had been executed by the Red Army. Johann's youngest sister Helene was already well into middle age, when she and her husband and son were roused in the middle of the night by Russian soldiers. The soldiers took her husband and son away, and she never saw them again.

Fanni's family above, Johann's below

I wrote to Tante Rudi, Fanni's niece, to ask what happened to her during the war. She wrote back that she married on the same day Hitler declared war in 1939. Their wedding portrait, on the right of composite, shows the worry and care of the day written on their faces. Her husband was a major in the gendarmerie, a peacetime police force that functioned as military police and conducted espionage during World War II. She gave birth to her oldest daughter, Ingrid, that same year and had a second daughter, Renate, in 1943.

In the last year of the war, she had to leave Vienna with her two girls, to stay on her uncle's farm in Niederoesterrich. Her husband remained on duty in Vienna and she did not hear from him for a long time. In the country, Tante Rudi and her girls had food to eat. She found work on farms. The local farmers, she writes, were astounded at how well a city gal like her took to such hard work.

"After the war was over, everything was destroyed. There wasn't much going on," so she and her girls didn't join her husband in Vienna until 1948. In her letter, Tante Rudi still remembers how Fanni, Johann, Margaret and her husband Johnny were a great help to them during the war. "We got a package before Christmas that I cannot express my gratitude for. I still think about it," she wrote in 1999, over 50 years later.

Fanni and Johann's move to America saved them from hardships that would have been in store for them in Vienna, if they had stayed. They were Catholics, but that was no guarantee of immunity from the Nazi's. For example, I have a friend who was born to a Catholic mother, in a forced labor farm. Usually babies born in camps did not survive. But miraculously, my friend's life was saved, because her mother made arrangements with the woman in charge to smuggle her baby out of camp to a foster mother, who cared for her until the war was over, and she could go get her.

My mother writes that Fanni "was grateful she and Johann and their daughters were spared the ravages of the Second World War." But they had to stand helplessly by and watch what happened to their brothers and sisters, in silent horror. Mom adds,

> Every so often, an ominous black-framed envelope would come in the mail from Austria during those World War II years, announcing another death in her family in Austria. If she cried over this, she did so in private, because I never heard her.

> Instead, she busied herself with collecting stuff for the Care packages she sent over toward the end of the war. She was grateful she was in a position to help her family in Austria during the war and afterward, sending over food and clothing.

Care Packages

Fanni assembled items that were hard to get in Austria, and shipped them to her sisters and brothers in Europe. She sent them things like coffee, canned ham, canned butter, sugar, and chocolate. Her packages were similar to the ones prepared by C.A.R.E. - The Cooperative for American Remittances to Europe. Americans could purchase C.A.R.E. boxes filled with goodies, starting in 1946, and have them sent to their family members still in Europe. Fanni made her own.

Friends and neighbors helped Fanni in this effort, bringing stuff over to the house to go into the packages. During the war, these packages had to go through USO channels, marked with an inventory for customs, which Margaret wrote out in her beautiful handwriting. When they were opened and inspected on the other side of the Atlantic, some items disappeared, like coffee, which was very hard to get in Europe, since it had to be imported in the first place from hot climates like Africa or South America.

Fanni also put second hand clothes and dry goods in the packages. Their boarder Herman had access to remnant yard goods, at his job as a security guard at the Jack Winter clothing factory. They allowed him to take what he wanted from a stash of things they weren't going to use any more. Every day he'd come home with a big load of thread, needles, remnants and sewing notions, things you could make clothing from. I still have a little match box of gauze butterflies that he got from there and they are so pretty, I've never been able to bring myself to actually sew them on anything.

Fanni's Kids Visit Europe

In her will, Fanni left Mom and Margaret the money that the City had paid her for her house, which they tore down for urban renewal. The idea behind the inheritance was that her daughters would visit Vienna and greet her remaining relatives for her. So Mom's first tour of Austria in the 70's was a kind of pilgrimage to meet Fanni's family. "They didn't have much money," Mom recalls, "but they sure were nice!"

I love Mom's account of her visit to Fanni's youngest brother, Onkel Johann [lower left on composite]. Their arrival was delayed by a day, when Johnny accidentally ran over his wife Margaret's foot. She missed the entire tour, because she stayed in the hospital, where at least she was exceptionally well taken care of. They couldn't call Onkel Johann to let him and his wife know they were still coming, because he didn't have a phone. Here are Mom's diary notes:

> We arrived a day late, at 5 in the afternoon, to find that Onkel Johann was napping. When he woke up, it took him a little while to realize we were actually there. Once Onkel had woken up completely, he was very pleased and excited to see us. His wife Tante explained that even though they had expected us the day before, they were still wearing their best clothes anyway, just in case we were still coming.

> Onkel is 91 years old. He looks a lot like Fanni. He moves slowly, but is still "lustig," [funny and cheerful] and has a twinkle in his eye. At 82, Tante Aloysia, his second wife, is energetic and hard-working. With Onkel, she is patient and very caring. They live simply and modestly in an upper apartment with a living room and bedroom. Outside the apartment down the hall, there is a shared kitchen. It you wanted to cook anything, you had to take it down there. Quite a ways down the same hall is a bathroom, also shared.

In spite of their modest lifestyle, they had a feast waiting for their American relatives.

Johnny helping Onkel Johann call Margaret

Betty and Mom at Fanni's apartment in Vienna

Onkel brought out a big bottle of Gumpoldskirchner wine, from a famous wine district in Austria by the same name, with a wine-making tradition pre-dating the Roman occupation. Tante served a fine schinken (smoked ham) and a beautiful, big torte, with excellent Jacobs-Kronung Kaffee. She said she had told the shopkeepers she needed the very best food for her American visitors. And it certainly was!

> After supper, Onkel told us what happened to him in 1945. He had been living in the family home in Sitzgras, the farm where Fanni was been born.   With no warning, the Russians invaded the town at 2:30 a.m., waking them up in the middle of the night. The Red Army lined up the men of the village against the wall and said, "you will be shot within a half an hour if all the people aren't out!" Onkel and his first wife left with only the clothes they could put on their backs and two pillows. By 3:00 a.m. the entire village of Sitzgras was evacuated.   His only children, two sons, were both killed in the war. Onkel survived the hardships of two world wars. We cannot begin to comprehend.

Onkel Johann was a displaced person, now living in Germany.

> The next day we had our regular pension breakfast and a second breakfast at Onkel's. Then we went outside to a phone booth, so Onkel could talk to Margaret, recuperating in the hospital. He had never used a phone before. Johnny got Margaret on the phone and handed it to Onkel.   He said "Guten Tag." Then he heard

her voice and he dropped the phone. He was so scared he wouldn't talk into the receiver.

Onkel Johann gave them 6 bottles of wine, 200 marks (which is a lot of money), torte, kuchen and cherries. Even though they had never met her before, Mom was showered with money and gifts by all of her mother's and father's relatives, in thanks for those packages that Fanni had sent. I think Mom came out ahead financially on that trip.

In 2004, I got to meet my Tante Rudi, Fanni's niece, the gal who had gone to the country with her girls Ingrid and Renate during the war. In preparation for the trip to Vienna, I learned a little German, mostly from my Mother. It was a good thing I did, because ten minutes after my cousin Renate brought us to her house, where her mother Tante Rudi lived, Renate and my Mom left to go shopping for a couple of hours. They left me with my 91 year old Tante Rudi, who didn't speak any English. Tanti Rudi sat me down and showed me how to play canasta - in German. The next day, after we polished off Renate's Wienerschnitzel, which was so big, it hung off our plates, Tante Rudi drew some cute little drawings, to teach me some handy words in German. She was very nice to me, but I could see her taxing her long-suffering daughter Renate, with criticism and demands.

Fanni also sent Care packages to Rosa Theimer and her family, who were good friends of Fanni, Johann and Margaret. Once time, Fanni sent them a christening gown (probably my mother's) and a brand new outfit for Rosa's baby brother, Roland. Rosa had actually kept that little outfit of Roland's, which she reverentially showed my mother when Mom visited 30 years later, in the 70's. "It was so beautiful," Rosa said glowingly. "It was the only new thing we owned for a long time."

Rosa hosted Mom, Johnny and Betty in Vienna in high style. Mom wrote in her travel diary,

> She always putting out her best china and freshly ironed linens and plenty of orange juice for us Americans. [The Apricosenkuchen recipe she made for them is included in Desserts] Rosa doesn't speak English, but she is a very warm, exuberant, expressive person and we had no trouble communicating with her, because she expresses herself not only with words, but with her eyes, hands, and every part of her body.

Thirty years after Mom's first trip to Vienna, I met Rosa myself on that 2004 trip with my mother. By this time, Rosa was in her 80's, but was still *lustig*. She had a little ash colored hair mixed in with her gray and wore her hair bobbed with two combs at the side of her head, just like Fanni did.

We were all out seeing the sights one day, when my cousin Ingrid was pickpocketed on the subway platform. While we waited for Ingrid to get a copy of her driver's license at the police station in the subway, next to a young pack of drug addicts lolling in front of the entrance to the station, Rosa regaled us with her urban tips, in German. Rosa acted out the action for me, my Mother and Renate. She pulled her pants pocket inside out, explaining, "I pin my house key to the inside of my pocket," showing us how she did it with a big safety pin. Then she explained, "I never carry a purse, just a little money, here, in my other pants pocket," fishing out a few bills and showing them to us. Next, she gave a knock to her head with her fist, that was comical. "Car crashes and big diseases that take you to the Kronkenhaus, [hospital] - these are something to be concerned about. But the loss of money is not such a big problem.   You just get some more money and the problem is solved!" Rosa was my kind of gal.

I was amazed at how new everything looked in Vienna, like it had just been built yesterday.   But Vienna was heavily bombed in World War II.   A look at the movie *The Third Man* will show you just what a rubble pile it was after the war, because that movie was shot on location in Vienna right after the war.

When the Nazis had retreated and the Russians invaded Vienna, the city was ablaze with fires that burned out of control for days.   The firefighters were all gone, having been drafted into the German army at the last minute.   Then the worst happened: the City's main cathedral, Stephansdom, was torched, either by the Russians or by looters, depending on whose account you believe.   The stained glass windows crashed to the floor.   When the roof fell in, an enormous bell called Die Pummerin, also crashed to the floor and broke into pieces.   When the fire was finally put out, the only stained glass remaining was the big rosette window in the back of the church.   The church lay open to the elements.   Even though the Viennese were completely broke after the war, they managed to chip in to build their Stephansdom a new roof, tile by tile.   Even Margaret and Johnny bought two tiles.

Many people call Stephansdom the "Heart of Vienna," and I found out why one afternoon, when I visited the cathedral, with my cousins Ingrid and Renate, my Mom and Rosa.   We were walking down a busy street in downtown Vienna.   I remember seeing a pretty girl dressed up in a man's 18th century frilly jacket and shirt, with a three cornered hat, standing on a street corner, handing out a sheet for that night's Mozart opera.   I wondered if I could get a job doing that.   Then a handsome Swiss guy in a business suit knocked into me with his brief case, when I wouldn't make way for him on the sidewalk. My Mother, Rosa and cousins didn't notice because they were jabbering away. They only glanced at him as he apologized profusely in German, bowing as he backed away.

Suddenly an archway yawned on the left. We slipped through it and found ourselves, walking across the cobblestones of Stefansplatz, towards an enormous black cathedral, Stephansdom, with its zigzag patterned roof. As soon as I spotted it, I was stunned and stopped in my tracks. My Mom and cousins backtracked to bring me along and we all went into the church together. Inside, Stephansdom was magical and mystical. Tears rolled down my face. My cousin Ingrid took me firmly by the arm and didn't let go the entire time we were there. We all sat down in a pew in silence. I wept in the presence of something ancient and familiar.

When Mom and I flew back to America, I had to wrestle a coifed and perfumed Air France agent to the ground. I needed to get my Mother a seat with leg room, so she could travel comfortably with her foot elevated, because she had acquired a leg infection in Vienna. Over the course of an hour, I tried reasoning with the lady-like agent, but that didn't work. I tried getting tough with her. That didn't work, either. I tried playing on her sympathy. "Wouldn't you want your mother to have extra leg room if she were traveling with cellulitus?" I demanded.

"I have no muzzer," she replied, defensively.

"Oh, great," I thought to myself. Still, I kept at her, with one strategy after another. Finally, after an hour she relented. I still don't know what it was that made her give my "muzzer" the seat assignment she needed.

Renate took my Mom into the bathroom and gave her the injection that the doctor had ordered, so Mom wouldn't get a blood clot from the cellulitis while she was flying. Once we said goodbye to Renate, got on the plane and Mom was safely tucked away in the rear of the plane with her leg up, I took my own seat, amidships. I was relieved, finally, that I didn't have to wrangle with either that ticket agent, or my Mother, who disapproved of the whole procedure. She was embarrassed, because I had "made waves" with the ticket agent and the flight attendant.

Then woman in the seat next to mine turned to me, smiling, and said something that blew me away. "Just because your mother is in the back of the plane pouting about getting special treatment, doesn't mean you didn't do the right thing."

Wow! She was an American and her name was Frances. We had a conversation about what I had gone go through to get the Air France agent to understand how important it was to give my Mother a seat with extra leg room. Frances defended my actions saying, "People react strongly to a strong woman. If they call you 'tough' it's only because they are used to seeing fawning women." Wow! I felt like I had sat down next to an angel!

How did sweet, loveable Fanni get a kick-ass granddaughter like me? At least both of Fanni's grandnieces, my Viennese cousins Ingrid and Renate, think it's cool they have an artist cousin in America!

"Do you like art?" I asked Frances. She nodded. I fished slides of my Taliesin paintings out of my bag and handed them to her. It was great sitting next to someone so wise, who also liked artwork. She particularly liked the *Statue with Staircase*, making this remarkable interpretation of my painting:

> With our messy, horrible, painful lives we create our heaven. In this painting, each step up is another painful experience we have lived through. We are all alone before God, in life, like the statue. The staircase is a conundrum, as it goes from the outside, out to the outside, just as in life our goal is to find the impossible but most workable route as we reach for the light.

Taliesin, Statue with Staircase

Stephansdom in 1905, when it still had all its stained glass

Margaret, Johann, Mom and Fanni, 1928

Chapter 10

Mehlspeise

[literally "flour eats"]

Sweet dishes for lunch or a light dinner

Genevieve Davis

French Toast Tuesdays

On Tuesdays, Fanni came out to our house on the bus to spend time with us, and to iron and mend our clothes. The night before, Mom came looking to see if I had any socks with holes in them, so Fanni would have some work to do, with her wooden egg and darning needle.

School was stifling. After a morning of being publicly humiliated, I opened the door to our house and walked into a wonderfully fragrant cloud of French toast cooking. I rushed into the kitchen, and found Fanni standing at the stove in an apron, fork in hand, turning over golden brown, half slices of bread overflowing with thick batter, her cheeks rosy from the heat. I threw my arms around her waist and buried my face in her cotton dress and apron. *Home safe.*

Reluctantly, I returned to school in the afternoon, but fortified by Grandma's French Toast. Sometimes at the end of the school day, I came home and watched her wistfully from the window. She was standing at the bus stop, along with the dark skinned women, who also ironed and mended in our suburb. A few minutes later, the bus would come and take Fanni away from me, back to the inner city with the other ladies.

French Toast, Viennese Style

Codified by Mom

5 slices of stale bread

2 eggs

1 cup milk

½ cup flour

sugar

jelly

cooking oil or butter

Cut stale bread into halves. Beat 2 eggs with ¼ to ½ cup milk. Add flour gradually to make a batter the consistency of heavy cream. Melt butter or cooking oil in frying pan. Dip bread into the batter and sauté on both sides in butter or oil, until golden brown. The first side down in the pan should dribble over the edge of the slice of bread, so you have a little extra cooked batter, attached to the French toast.

We either sprinkled granulated sugar on our French toast, or spread a thick, jewel-like layer of Fanni's jelly on it.

Brot Schmarren or Kaiserschmarren
(the Crumbs of the Czar)

This was a favorite of the Emperor Franz Josef, the ruler of the Austro-Hungarian Empire. Johann was fond of him as a leader. The Emperor had humble tastes, which included not only enjoying this left over bread dish, but also sleeping on a military cot in his office.

My friend Tea, from the former Yugoslavia, which was once part of the Austro-Hungarian Empire, knows this dish as "Carske Mrvice." We went camping together and flipped pancakes on our little camp cookware sets over a propane flame. If they fell apart, she would dub them "Carske Mrvice." We'd drown them in maple syrup and wolf them down with gusto, in the pines and open air, before dashing off to rock climb at Devils Lake!

Stale bread

French toast batter

Cooking oil or butter

Sliced Apples [optional]

Powdered sugar and cinnamon

Take stale bread and tear into pieces. Dip in French toast batter. Pan sauté in butter or oil of your choice. You can fry up peeled apple slices in the pan at the same time. Serve up all with powdered sugar and cinnamon sprinkled on top.

Crepes
also called Palatschinken or Omletten

Codified by Mom

This the Viennese way to make a meal with flour and egg and a little milk. Grandma called them "roll ups."

4 cups flour

3 to 4 eggs

3 cups milk, or more for thin crepes

a little salt – 1 tsp.

butter or oil to cook the crepes in

jelly

powdered sugar

Mix egg, milk, flour and salt. Drop this liquidy batter to make one crepe at a time on a hot skillet coated with butter or oil. Spread with jelly and roll up. Then, sprinkle with powdered sugar. Grandma made these one by one and served it to the lucky one whose turn was next! Alternatively, you can make them all ahead, keep them warm in a slow oven, and serve them all at the same time.

Jelly

Our back yard, where currents, raspberries, grapes, and plums grew, was a source for all kinds of jellies that Fanni made. Mom soaked the labels off of glass peanut butter jars, then Fanni used them in her canning. A new, tiny label in Fanni's friendly handwriting told us what kind of fruit she had put inside, and sealed with a big wax plug on the top.

Her jelly recipe came right off of the Sure-Gel box. How American! Mom used the same recipe, yet their jellies tasted quite different. All of us, Mom included, preferred Fanni's. I hope yours tastes as good, following the directions on the box!

Fanni waving goodbye as we drive away from her apartment

My Rootin' Tootin' Raspberry Jam

I once lived in a house where I had raspberry bushes in the backyard. One year they gave double berries. I made this raspberry jam that Mom said was even better than Fanni's. Oh! That's high praise!

2 qts. Raspberries

3C Honey

5 C Sugar [you could try using a lot less]

1 Package Sure-Gel

½ Lemon – juiced

1 Carton paraffin

Sterilize:

Metal Spoon

Ladle

Jars

Lids

Mix honey and sugar over heat to boiling, about 10 minutes. Add Sure-Gel and stir until dissolved.

Add fruit. Bring to a boil that can't be stirred down for 1 minute. Cool and skim for 5 minutes.

Ladle into jars. Seal with ½ " paraffin as you go. When jam is cool, seal again with another 1/8" paraffin.

My Health Food Crepes

½ cup brown rice flour (white is okay, too)

2 heaping T flax meal or seeds

water or milk or almond milk to moisten

farm egg with a nice orange yolk

salt to taste

flax oil or your favorite oil

This makes one serving of crepes with a delightful taste and smell. Beat the egg. Mix the flour, flax and salt together with the egg and the water or milk to make a runny batter.

Heat a skillet to a medium low heat. Pour 1 tsp to 1 T of flax oil (or your favorite oil if flax is too fishy for you) into an iron skillet and quickly pour batter in for one crepe.   Makes about 3 crepes that are very stiff.   Serve with cinnamon or honey or chopped fruit or jelly.

Potato Pancakes

Codified by Mom

2 cups potatoes

2 eggs

salt

pinch of baking powder

chopped onion

1 T flour

oil or butter for frying

Soak potatoes in water for several hours to make crispy (optional step). Drain and grate. Beat eggs and mix together with potatoes, adding a little pepper. Drop into a pan with 1/8 inch hot oil or butter. Alternatively, fry at 400 degrees on an electric frying pan. Cook until brown on one side. Turn and brown the other. Drain on paper towels.

Serve with applesauce on the side or on top.

Fanni & Johann's house on 16th Street

Applesauce

In September, we climbed up into the apple tree and picked all the fruit hanging from the branches that we could reach. We also picked up the ones that looked pretty good from the ground. Then Fanni sat on a pad on our back stoop and carved up apples with a paring knife, cutting out the bits of fruit that weren't wormy from our tree. Sometimes there'd be just a little piece left of the apple, after she had patiently cut the wormy parts out of them. Those she cooked up for applesauce, adding a little sugar and sometimes cinnamon.

Apples

Water

Sugar

Cinnamon

Peel and core apples. Cut into slices. Put in a pan and cover with water. Bring to a boil, then turn heat down and simmer about 10 minutes, until apples fall apart. Put through a ricer. Or buzz in your food processor. Add sugar and cinnamon to taste.

My Variation on Fanni's Applesauce

Apples

Spring or well water

Cinnamon [optional]

Cut up apples and core, leaving the skins on, if the apples are unsprayed. Put in a pan and cover with water. Bring to a boil. Turn off heat. Pour apples and water into a food processor and buzz up until peels are pureed. Sprinkle cinnamon, if desired, on top when you serve it.

My Raw Applesauce

Apples

Spring or well water

You don't really need to cook apples to make applesauce. This recipe preserves the enzymes in the fruit, to benefit your digestion.

Cut up apples and core. Leave the skins on if the apples are unsprayed. Put in a food processor and cover with water. Buzz for several minutes, until peels are pureed.

Spaetzle or Drop Noodles

Codified by Mom

2 quarts of boiling water

1 T oil

2 tsp. salt

2 cups flour

½ tsp. salt

¼ tsp. nutmeg

2 eggs

½ to ¾ cup milk

Pour water into a pot and add 1 T oil and 2 tsp salt and bring to a boil.

Meanwhile, sift together flour, salt and nutmeg. Beat in eggs. Add some of the milk, gradually, beating to make a heavy dough, until it comes easily from side of the bowl.

Use a teaspoon to drop small bits of the batter into the boiling water. Return to a boil and simmer 6 – 8 minutes, stirring occasionally. Drain, dash with cold water.

If desired, sauté spaetzle in 2 T butter until golden and sprinkle with toasted bread crumbs.

Noodles and Crumbs

Codified by Margaret

2 cups egg noodles

2 T butter or olive oil

salt and pepper to taste

1 or 2 T chopped parsley

½ cup bread crumbs

3 T butter

Drain noodles and mix with butter, salt and parsley. Brown bread crumbs in remaining butter in a large skillet. Add noodles and mix until coated. Sprinkle with sugar and cinnamon.

Milch Reis or Milk Rice

Grandma used to make this for me for a light dinner.

¼ cup milk

1 cup white cooked rice

a little flour

¼ cup raisins

cinnamon

sugar

In a saucepan, combine milk, white cooked rice and a little flour, and heat over a low flame. Sprinkle with cinnamon and sugar. Add ¼ cup of raisins. Stir while heating until rice is hot and coated.

I love this picture of my Mother, selling tickets in the booth at the Varsity Theater. I came across this picture when I was making arrangements for a screening of my film, **Secret Life, Secret Death**, with the manager of the Rosebud Theater, on North Avenue in Milwaukee. When I mentioned that my Mother used to be a glamorous secretary at Fox Theaters, the theater manager, who had written a book on the history of movie theaters in Milwaukee, said, "I think I have a picture of your mother in my book." He opened it, and there was this pic of Mom at the second anniversary showing of The Wizard of Oz, which was released in 1941.

That dates the picture as being taken in 1942. Mom worked in the ticket booth at the Varsity when she was in secretarial school in 1942. She was "spotted" there by one of the higher-ups and was brought upstairs to work in their offices, when she finished her course work. Oh yeah, the guy in the insert, which comes from my friend's book, is Mr. X.

Chapter 11

Fanni and Mom

Moving Violation

When we were kids and wrecked something, Fanni scolded us, "Shame on you! Look what you've done!" That is exactly the same treatment a police officer got, when he wrote my mother a traffic ticket in 1958.

It was 4:00 am and still dark out, when Mom, Fanni and Margaret headed out of Milwaukee, on their way to the funeral of Kathi, Fanni's sister-in-law. It was the middle of the night and Mom was driving Dad's old Packard, because neither Fanni nor Margaret had ever learned to drive. After Mom drove through a huge, dark, empty intersection under construction, a police car came up behind them with a screeching siren and whirling red lights. Mom pulled over. In the darkness, a police officer emerged from the car and wrote out a ticket for being in the wrong lane in a construction zone. He handed it to my Mother, and she immediately burst into tears, behind the steering wheel.

Sitting in the back seat, wearing her Sunday dress, good coat and hat, Fanni leaned forward and shook her finger at the police officer. "How could you do such a thing? Shame on you!" she scolded him. Look at what you've done! She has to drive us all the way to Baraboo for a funeral and you've made her so upset, she can't even drive! "

The officer listened to Fanni, speechless. Then he hung his head. What else could he do? He tore up the ticket.

Mom perched on Dad's car

Another Rescue

As my mother tells it, Fanni "saved me from a monster."

When Mom was a young, lovely girl just out of high school, she got a plum job as a glamorous secretary to the Milwaukee President of Fox Theaters in the early 1940's. The company had a whole chain of theaters in Wisconsin and Upper Michigan. That's back when movie theaters were part of the same companies that produced films, before federal court anti-trust action put an end to it in 1948. The Milwaukee Fox office had direct connections to Hollywood, bringing through such greats as Roy Rogers *and* his horse Trigger, both of whom my mom got to meet in person. Rogers actually invited Mom to his dressing room, so he could serenade her. She accepted his invitation, bringing along two of her girlfriends, just in case he had any funny business in mind. They all crowded into his dressing room and listened to him croon songs, while accompanying himself on his guitar.

When Mom was studying in a year-long secretarial skills program, she started out working for Fox, as an usherette at the Varsity Theater on Wisconsin Avenue. After the movie started, she escorted patrons to their seats, with a flashlight to light the way in the darkened theater. Back then, every seat had an ashtray attached to it, because you could smoke during the movie. During intermission between shows on double feature nights, Mom had to put on a box that hung from her shoulders and sell cigarettes, candy and soda. She didn't like that part of the job. But the rest of it was great, because she got to watch a lot of movies.

Then she was promoted to ticket seller in the little glass booth outside the theater. "I loved that," Mom remembers.

The Bevy of secretaries. Mom is third from the left

Mom in the upper left in the lounge at Fox

I got to see movie stars that came to visit Fox's corporate offices upstairs. They would arrive in a limo in front of my booth, get out and talk to somebody from upstairs, right in front of where I was working.

Soon after that I was "spotted" and brought upstairs. Part of my job as a secretary was to entertain by serving cocktails and snacks when they adjourned a meeting. Sometimes I worked doing that 'til 10 at night. And sometimes I worked til 3 a.m. with the boss, taking dictation in shorthand and typing up things. Then I walked home. It was safe to walk the streets there back then and it wasn't far from my house.

It was about a mile and a half away from 20th and Highland. The President, a tall, tanned attractive man of about 50, with a trim physique and an elegant shock of white hair, was a lady killer who knew just what effect he had on women. According to Mom, he had a large office suite that took up the whole top floor of the building. It included a cocktail lounge, a kitchen, a liquor room with hundreds of bottles of Cutty Sark in it, his own shower, a small movie theater, several conference rooms, a dressing room, a massage room where he would also tan under a sun lamp and a couch that converted into a bed.

"He had eight receptionists who answered the phones in his office," Mom explains. "Several of them - I don't know what they did for him. He took them on trips. Some were *capable*," Mom says, "and some were just for show. There were two secretaries who actually did the office work." One of those capable ones was Mom. She was beauty *and* brains, a combination that continually confounded her employer. Her boss tried several times to maneuver her into a vulnerable situation over the two-year period of time she worked for him. "Only single girls were allowed to work as secretaries," Mom recalls. "They were asked to leave when they got married, because of the possible nuisance of pregnancies!"

Mom told me that working for the boss was always interesting.

> The President was involved in a lot of things. He was the head guy for contributing to the war effort. So I got to meet a lot of senators and mayors, and big wigs from the Milwaukee area, who would come to discuss what they could do for the servicemen. And he was always going back and forth between Los Angeles and New York.

"Office gossip about his inter-office romances, and his affairs with certain movie actresses when they came to visit, circulated widely during coffee break," Mom continues. "He had quite a few movie actresses who were in love with him. They would call and want to talk to him and I would be the one to take the calls. The actress Carole Landis was in love with him."

After Mom told me that, I researched Landis's life and she has many points of connection to Mr. X's world. She was a native of Wisconsin. She did major movie roles in the early 40's, under contract with 20ᵗʰ Century Fox. Also, she was a USO entertainer and a popular pin-up with the servicemen, that Mr. X got involved helping in his meetings with local bigwigs. And she had a penchant for relationships with men in charge, like Broadway producer Busby Berkeley, as well as Mr. X, who enjoyed the perks of being a big fish in a small pond.

premiere at fox wisconsin reveals new theatre of tomorrow

by george spelvin, jr.

I N THESE PAGES you have read of the precedent-shattering type of production 20th Century Fox has brought to Wisconsin this April of 1950.

However, your correspondent would like to describe to you the setting of this history-making entertainment — a theatre that forebodes what Mr. and Mrs. America will know in the tomorrow of the theatre, and truly we have tonight sat in that theatre. We were conducted through this modern edifice by Mr. H. J. Fitzgerald, President of the Fox Wisconsin Amusement Corporation, who constructed and operate this temple of tomorrow.

Vocal Canopy

As we approached Fox Wisconsin we were attracted by a unique canopy lighting wherein against the background of rainbow-hued colors a running televised message of approximately 50 words, embellished on either side by the neon-outlined faces of the stars, told us in a moment what was currently playing— and then, much to our optical amazement, the message disappeared and in a background of music a well-modulated voice told us not only what was currently playing, but related up-to-the-moment international news. Truly we were greeted from the stars, with the most modern of announcements, visual, colorful, and vocal.

Air-conditioned Sidewalk

And we had no sooner reached the front of the theatre when we learned that through a mechanical arrangement soft warm air is exuded which makes possible the sidewalk free of snow and ice in the wintertime while in summertime cool air flows for comforting purposes.

Triple Box Office

The front of the theatre displayed not one, but three box offices; one in the center and two on either side. Though not all three were in service, the two on the sides were arranged as movable display signs.

Scent Control

With all these surprising innovations, we were greeted upon entering the theatre by an exhilarated tingle. An atmosphere of gardenias permeated the air. This not only was pleasing to the sense of smell but we found that this had a healthsitical effect. This not only gives a pleasant effect but cleanses and healthifies and kills all bacteria. We entered directly from the outer entrance into the auditorium foyer without a set of second doors. The new control of heating and lighting eliminates the necessity of the obsolete set of doors.

Projecting off on either side of the theatre were two Service Center Arcades which permitted the doorman to take tickets not only from the front doors but from those patrons entering from the arcades.

Arcade Annex

This arcade is arranged for the greatest comfort of transient and current customers. The arcades provide a florist shop, beauty parlor, barber shop, cosmetic counter, delicatessen, ladies' accessory shop, dentist's office, and plate lunch shop. Alluringly displayed in the ladies' accessory shop are jewelry creations that are worn in the current picture being shown and previews of novelty pieces that will soon be seen on the screen. There is a merchandis-

Featured in the innovating show which premiered at the Fox Wisconsin theatre last night, was lovely CELESTE ORCHIDE who has the first seven-way contract in Hollywood, having been awarded this all-inclusive contract after the international premiere by Mr. T. J. Connors. Miss Orchide will be featured in many future all TELEVISION, all THIRD DIMENSION, all SCENTED, all NATURAL COLOR, and all SINGING pictures.

ing department in the lobby for edibles, vending holiday novelties, and an attractive display with quaint signs and also carrying novelties that will first appear in the forthcoming attraction.

In the midst of these attractive displays in the arcade there appears a constant corps of models displaying the newest creations which are worn in the current picture.

Accommodation Desk

In the middle of the arcade we come across a marble white counter in back of which is a pleasant and competent attendant. Here, for a nominal fee, we can obtain general information and checking service. Information includes shopping news, the latest train schedules, and plane reservations can be made. The general information answers all types of queries. Our lady of the evening told us later that in the powder room there is an annex with all modern accessories. Shower baths and dressing rooms are provided, and for a nominal fee a working girl can change for the evening's social engagements.

Balcony Escalators

This new theatre has overlooked no comfort or convenience to the patron. Those who prefer a favorite seat in the balcony or side tiers, have but to ascend

in a multi-hued escalator to the tune of soft, tingling music.

But to the auditorium — where we had our seats — this, too, was a revelation. There were no draperies — soft lighting and spun glass conveyed a decorative effect. The lighting system of the auditorium synchronizes with the screen so that the mood of the picture is transmitted to the auditorium of the theatre in color as was the musical background, and attuned with the floral picture various flower scents permeated throughout the theatre.

Multi-aisles

As one sauntered down these wide, spacious aisles—more aisles than seen in any theatre—Mr. H. J. Fitzgerald explained to us that these numerous aisles made it convenient for the patrons to leave the theatre without disturbing the others. These wide aisles tied-in with the service plan arrangement, for on the back of each seat ahead of each patron there is a button which afforded the patron any service he may desire. The comfortable chairs themselves provided relaxation for patrons while viewing the picture.

Fluorescent Directionals

Fluorescent directional signs on the floor as well as designated markers eliminated the need for ushers. However, the service attendants were ever at hand, though quiet and unobserved.

Seasonal Side Panels

On either side of the auditorium, special lighting effects were noticed. In the summer, sandy seashores were depicted and the lighting effects created the illusion of waves washing up on the shore. Sailboats could be seen in the distance, behind which rose snow-capped mountains. In winter this arrangement is changed by a simple adjustment of the auditorium panels. Small palm trees actually seem to blow in the soft breeze against the same background of summer.

For purposes of added convenience and comfort to the patrons, a small paneled compartment on the back of the seat ahead pulls forward and reveals a special compartment for hats, purses, gloves, coats, or packages.

Rubberized Carpet

One becomes conscious that there is no carpeting on the floors of this modern theatre—fluorescent designs on rubber concrete provide decorative effects. Mr. Fitzgerald explains that a simple water spray in the rear of the theatre makes cleaning of the theatre thorough and speedy by a flush system from this fine spray. Our attention is caught by the back section of the theatre which provided a mild sun lamp treatment for those who wished while viewing the picture. Another section was provided especially for the hard of hearing.

Seating Control Board

We thought we had run out of innovation but while leaving the theatre we observed the chief service attendant before a huge board with a myriad of buttons—a seating plan of the theatre. As a patron left his seat, the slight pressure lighted the button on the board so that at a glance he could direct incoming patrons.

The theatre of 1950? Yes, we had been in it—the theatre of tomorrow at Fox Wisconsin!

Mom in a Publicity Stunt for Smell-O-Rama Movies

Mom herself had a dream to go out to Hollywood to become an actress. There was another gal at the office, with a lot of personality, who did just that. Mom elaborates:

> One receptionist I worked with was so funny, Patty. She lived nearby in a mansion on Highland Boulevard. She had a great sense of humor and like to play practical jokes. If I was out of the office when she stopped by, she would put my wastebasket on top of my neatly ordered desk or something else silly like that. We had a lot of fun together. She was smart because she worked for the vice president as his secretary, doing real work, and she was the only one in that office. They had a romance and were together for a long time.
>
> Then she went out to Hollywood, where she got a part in the circus movie, *Trapese* with Burt Lancaster. She was gorgeous and looked like Hollywood actress, Heddy Lamar. She played a circus performer in that movie, but her part wound up on the editing floor.

Mom told me that when Patty left for Hollywood, Mom was offered her executive secretary job with the Vice President. She took it. Why would she accept a demotion? Read on.

The president, (who, at Mom's request, I am calling "Mr. X"), according to Mom was, "an Adonis. So perfect. For me, it was an ideal job working for him." Yeah, that is, until he passed over all the secretaries who were not "capable," and singled out Mom to accompany him on a working trip from Wisconsin to Hollywood, on the train. That involved about 3 days in close quarters on the train. At night the seats in a Pullman car converted to berths for sleeping. Theoretically, a sleeping berth was supposed to be private, but the sleeper was only separated from the aisle by a curtain and really, anybody could climb in, in the middle of the night.

The night before they were scheduled to leave on the train for California, Mom had a bad stomachache. She had already decided not to go, because she knew what was up. But she says she was "scared to death to break the news to my boss." And now it was the last minute, the morning when they were supposed to leave. She told her mother what was the matter. So Fanni put on her coat and hat, and walked downtown to the Fox Theater offices that morning. She told Mr. X she would not allow him to take her daughter on such a trip.

After striking out with my Mom the first time, the president didn't give up. He would sometimes call on her to take notes during a meeting. Then, while she was busily taking down what was being said in shorthand, he would turn to her and ask sarcastically, "And what do you think, Miss Baier?" The man who dished out sarcasm wasn't immune to the same treatment himself, Mom explains. "People called the him 'the Great White Father' behind his back!"

Foiled in his transcontinental attempt, the boss later wanted Mom to accompany him to Chicago, on another working trip, to meet with Hollywood moguls down there. Mom elaborates:

> He needed a good secretary to take down his preparatory notes on the two-hour train ride, and to sit in the next day on the early morning conferences, taking notes. I could hardly refuse that and keep my job.

Mom missed the entertainment at Chez Paris

Ad for Chicago's Ambassador

But I must've looked scared, because he had me call to make a hotel reservation for him, and then make another one under my own name. Of course, that was no guarantee that all I had to do was take notes. He might have had an additional plan in mind.

Mom boarded the train with her boss, wearing her one, good, gray, woolen suit. In those days, a professional secretary only needed one expensive suit and just changed blouses as needed. After the two hour train ride, they went over to their rooms at the posh Ambassador Hotel in Chicago.

"In the early evening he walked with me up to the bar in the hotel. 'What would you like to drink?'" he asked." Mom didn't know how to answer. She was just a 19 year old girl and had never had a drink in a bar before. "Would you like a Manhattan?" Mr. X inquired.

Mom had seen plenty of movies where people drank Manhattans. She thought to herself, "A Manhattan! It sounds so sophisticated." So she said, "Yeah."

That's about all she remembers of the next several hours, except that she might have had another Manhattan and some dinner. A Manhattan is stronger than a double. It's made with 2 or more shots of whiskey, a little fortified wine, a splash of bitters and a cherry, for window dressing. It's pretty much the strongest drink you could order at the time. Next thing Mom knew, it was 10 p.m. and she was flat on her back on the bed in her room, fully clothed. Mr. X was knocking on the adjoining door, conveniently located between their rooms. He asked through the door, "Are you okay? If you're okay, I'm going to Chez Paris." *Chez Paris*? She had heard so much about what a glamorous place that was! Movie stars went there! So she peeled herself off the bed.

They took their places at a ringside table at *Chez Paris*, because Mr. X was well known at the club, and could get that kind of VIP service. About all Mom remembers about *Chez Paris* was that there was going to be an orchestra and dancers, and their table had a white table cloth on it. That's because about a minute after they were seated, she threw up all over that white table cloth. *And* her only suit. "About the time I sat down, *it* came up. I must have had some dinner earlier after the two Manhattans. I was mortified!"

The president took one look at her and shoved some bills in her hand, and told her to have the matron in the ladies' room clean her up, and then call herself a cab and go back to the hotel by herself. Good thing she missed the floor show, because *Chez Paris* was a burlesque club! Imagine Mom watching the girlies strip down to their pasties!

The next morning, Mom relates,

> I went to his suite to transcribe his notes before the meetings. My one good suit was the only thing I had to wear and it still reeked from the smell of vomit. Even I could smell it. He was so disgusted that he called for a cab to take me to the train station. I went home alone, leaving him high and dry again! My boss had had enough of a naive, young girl, who could type.

That's when Mom took the demotion to the Vice President's office. According to Mom, "He was not good looking at all. He was strictly business with me, so I felt safe."

> Dad went right along with that image of an Adonis, the same factor that Mr. X had. He was

Roy Rogers serenaded my Mom & her friends in his dressing room

suave, handsome, sophisticated, worldly, with a full head of hair. Dad was a statistician for Fox Theaters in Iron Mountain, Michigan. He came down here to Milwaukee for meetings. That's how we met. He had great ears, which I had a chance to observe when I sometimes sat behind him in staff meetings. A lot of times he would fall asleep, and Mr. X would call on him and quiz him on what was going on in the meeting. Dad always knew and could repeat back to Mr. X what he had just said.

When my Dad was in Milwaukee to do business, he lived at the beautiful, classic art deco Ambassador Hotel. During my parents' two and a half year engagement, they lead a glamorous nightlife in fancy clubs in Milwaukee and Chicago, and my Dad never once tried to get fresh with her.

The Fox Theater management, however, frowned on their employees dating the glamorous secretaries. When they found out Mom and Dad were sneaking around seeing each other, Mom says, "they put Dad to managing the Princess Theater on 3rd and Wells. The Princess was a sleazy 24 hour operation that had live burlesque between movies. It didn't work out for our romance, because he had no free time at night."

So Dad left Fox Theaters and went to work in Milwaukee as a salesman. Mom kept her job. But she says Dad kept "pushing and pushing me to quit Fox theaters, where I often worked late into the night. He didn't want me in that place anymore. 'I want to see you more,' he told me.

Finally, Mom left Fox when she got a lead, through the secretarial school she had gone to, about a job with some attorneys. It didn't require night work, but one of the lawyers continually chased her around the office, trying to kiss her. She worked for them for a year. Mom points out, "I was asked to leave when I married Dad. How's that for harassment and discrimination!"

During their long engagement, Mom also gave up her dream of going to Hollywood and trying to make it. Just imagine how long that would have lasted with all the deals made on the casting couch! She could have done well as a secretary in a movie studio, though, or the script girl or a casting agent. Instead, she married my Dad.

She thought Dad was a wealthy guy, blowing all that money on her on their nights out. But after the wedding, when Dad asked Mom to pay for their new furniture from her savings, Mom realized Dad wasn't rich. That's where the money she had saved to go out to Hollywood went. Apparently, Dad had been spending every penny he made on their nights out.

Then, after they were married, Mom was out with Dad, when they ran into Mr. X, at the elegant Empire Room of Milwaukee's old Schroeder Hotel. Mr. X offered to buy her another Manhattan. By this time, Mom had had a little more experience going to night clubs and knew how to nurse a long, tall, watered down drink for the whole night, so she wouldn't get bombed. But, for some reason she accepted the Manhattan from her ex-boss, and had another black out that night. The next day, Dad had to tell her that sometime later that evening, she had been introduced to well known band leader, Orrin Tucker. He had been playing at the Empire Room, and had come over to their table to meet them and chat with Mr. X. It was an exciting moment to meet a famous big band leader in person, but Mom couldn't recall any of it.

My parents out on the town. My Mom's hat was fuscia.

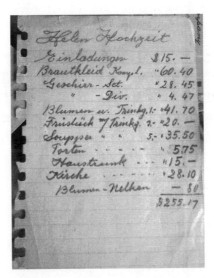

Johann wrote out this tally of Mom's wedding expenses

Fanni at the dining room table having dessert

Chapter 12

Desserts

.

Austrian Doughs

There is *Murbeteig*, which melts in your mouth. It's a dense, crumbly dough, like shortbread. It is used as a base for kuchen, in which it is piled with plums, apricots, or apples.

Another dough is called *Strudelteig*. It's amazingly thin. The dough is sprinkled with a filling, then rolled up, layer over layer into a log. Then it is baked and cut into slices. Mom points out that the dough does not merge with its filling, but remains independent of it. It is used in making Apfelstrudel. The way Grandma made it, it wasn't a flaky dough that melted in your mouth, but rather something you had to chew.

Biskuitteig is a sponge cake dough, which does not use leavening, but rather egg whites for its spongy texture. Biskuitteig, is made with only with eggs sugar, and flour. Find my cousin Renate's recipe for it under Strawberry Cake.

Then there is *Brandteig*, a boiled dough used for fruit dumplings. Made from eggs, milk, flour, salt. If you know French cuisine, they call it "choux." You can fry it, to make doughnuts. You can also bake it to make cream puffs, éclairs, etc. And boiled, it's an alternate dough for Plum Dumplings.

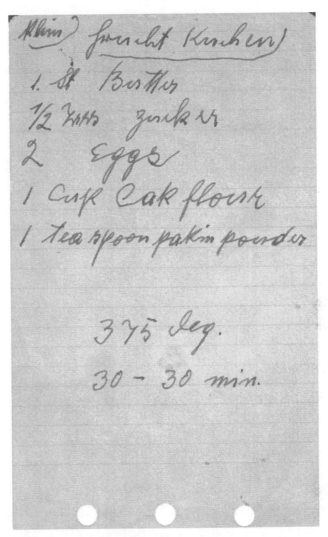

Fanni's Kuchen recipe

Genevieve Davis

Fanni's Klein Frucht Kuchen
Small Fruit Kuchen

Here is what Fanni used to make *Murbeteig*

1 Sk [stick] Butter

½ tass [cup] zucker

2 eggs

1 cup cak[e] flour

1 teaspoon pakim [baking] powder

I think the idea is you sift the flour, sugar and baking powder together. Add two beaten eggs and mix. Add melted butter and mix until the consistency is uniform.

Grease an oblong pan. Spread or press kuchen dough so it fills the bottom of the pan. Lay out slices of apples, plums, apricots or apples (or try any berries or pitted cherries) in parallel rows on top of the dough. Sprinkle with cinnamon and sugar. Bake at 375 degrees for 30 minutes with fruit on it.

Fresh Plum Kuchen

MEMORANDA

1 1/2 c sifted all purpose flour

2 t baking powder

3/4 t salt

1/4 c sugar

1/4 c butter

1 egg

3/4 c milk

Plum halves

1. Sift flour, baking powder, salt and sugar together. Cut in butter with pastry blender to resemble coarse meal.

2. Add blended egg and milk. Mix.

3. Pour into greased pan.

Topping

3/4 c sugar

1 T flour

1/2 t cinnamon

Bake at 400° about 30 min

Margaret's Kuchen recipe written out in her beautiful hand

Fresh Plum Kuchen

Codified by Margaret

Both Mom and Margaret's daughter Betty say this makes a better kuchen than Fanni's recipe.

1 ½ c sifted all purpose flour

2 t baking powder

¾ tsp salt

¼ c sugar

¼ cup butter

1 egg

¾ c milk

Plum halves with the pits removed

1. Sift flour, baking powder, salt and sugar together. Cut in butter with pastry blender to resemble coarse meal.
2. Add blended egg and milk mixture
3. Pour into greased pan

Arrange plum halves over dough.

Topping

¾ c sugar

1 T flour

½ t cinnamon

Mix together dry ingredients and sprinkle over the top of the plums.

Bake at 400 degrees about 30 min.

Apricots in Austria

Apricots, which grow well in the climate, are a favorite in Austrian cooking. Mom visited Fini at her home at Arsenale, where apricot trees grew on the grounds. Arsenale was built in 1848 as part of a complex of military buildings. You enter the apartment building through an enormous double door, tall enough to admit four men riding abreast on horseback.

"Fini's apartment is reached by climbing 124 steps to the fourth floor," Mom wrote in her travel diary, "where the hallways are very wide, with huge windows that overlook a courtyard, used during World War I for marching maneuvers." Then Nazi's took it over in World War II. Mom continues, "When we looked out the windows, we saw two American solders patrolling around a large storage-type building, so there is still something military going on at Arsenale, but nobody seemed to know what it was or seemed to be concerned about it. We saw the soldiers snitching and munching apricots off the trees while patrolling."

Mom writes, "At night, after dinner, we took a brisk walk around the Arsenale grounds. A full moon was out to welcome us on our first night in Vienna."

Probably it's the Viennese moonlight that makes the apricots taste so good!

Apricosenkuchen

From Rosa in Vienna

Rosa made this for Mom and then gave her the recipe. Rosa lives across the street from Fini. Like all Austrians, Rosa cooks by weight. If this recipe doesn't suit you, or if you don't have a kitchen scale, try using the plum kuchen recipe and substituting apricots for the plums

Murbeteig the Austrian Way:

Equal weight [*Gleichgewicht*] of eggs, flour, sugar.

Half weight [*Halbgewicht*] of oleo, [or try butter or oil]

A *Rampferl* of baking powder, which Mom says is a "pinch"

Halved apricots or other fruit, which you place on top of the *Murbeteig*. Bake at 350 degrees about 30 minutes.

Rosa, daughter of Fanni & Johann's friends in Vienna. Also Margaret's best friend when she lived in Vienna. Then Mom's friend. Lively, funny gal and a great cook!

Apfelstrudel

For Christmas Fanni made Apfelstrudel, a culinary masterpiece. Tart apples, cinnamon, sugar and raisins are tucked in, between layer upon layer of paper-thin pastry. According to my Mom, it was "an all day affair," but it's really more like just a few hours.

To begin, Fanni put the noodle board Johann had made on top of the kitchen table. The board measured 4' x 4', and was about an inch and a half thick, with a 3" edge on one side, so the dough didn't fall onto the floor.

First, she covered the board with a clean, cotton cloth. Then Fanni rolled out the dough, with the extra large wooden rolling pin Johann had made specifically for her Strudel-making. When she had rolled the dough out as far as it would go, Fanni called in my Mom and Margaret and one of the men. Everybody would take up a corner and pull it out gently, teasing it thinner and thinner, until gradually it spread over the entire noodle board. They pulled the dough out so thin you could read a newspaper through it.

Mom wrote in her travel diary, that Fanni's niece Fini made Strudel for them in Vienna. "It's a rare art to make Apfelstrudel in the old Viennese way and she certainly knew how to do it. It takes hours to make. And lots of effort, too. She said you have to slap the dough around hard for at least 15 minutes." Fanni kneaded hers, instead.

Strudelteig isn't too hard to make. It's fun to join in with the generations of ladies, who have made this since forever. Even though I watched Fanni do it, I never really learned until I tried out this recipe, which I reconstructed from eating her strudel and watching her as a kid. So give it a try!

Strudelteig

3 cups sifted flour

½ tsp. salt, sprinkled over the top

1 egg, beaten

1 T oil

1 cup lukewarm water, or slightly less

Place the sifted flour and salt in a bowl and form a well in the center. Add the beaten egg and the oil. Mix – you will have a lumpy, dry mixture. Gradually add water, until you have a soft, sticky dough.

Flour your hands and a kneading surface. Grab the dough out of the bowl and knead. Add flour as often as you need to, to keep it from sticking, which you will only need the first few minutes. Knead for 10 minutes. The dough will be soft and pliable. This kneading prepares the dough to be stretched paper-thin, so make sure you do the whole 10 minutes. Alternatively, you can slap the dough down hard, the way Fini did it, 100 to 125 times, for 15 minutes and then knead the dough a little. Place the dough in a bowl to rest for 30 minutes. Rub with butter and cover.

Apple Filling

6 medium sized apples

3 T or as much as 6 T sugar, depending on your sweet tooth

1 ½ T cinnamon

12 clove buds – just the crushed papery end

a good dash of nutmeg and optional 1 tsp. vanilla

Slice the apples into 1/8 slices. [You can leave the peels on if unsprayed] Put into a bowl and add the sugar and spices and toss. Toss again, while you make the rest of the filling.

Filling, Nuts

1 cup nuts, such as walnuts or hazelnuts

In a food processor, grind the nuts. You can grind them into a meal or leave them chunky.

Filling, Bread Crumbs

3/4 cup bread crumbs,

2 T butter

Make bread crumbs from a baguette or other flavorful bread, by tearing into shreds and drying by air or in a warm oven. Grind baguette to crumbs in a food processor.

Put the crumbs and butter into a frying pan and brown over a medium-low heat. Stir frequently to prevent burning.

Making the Strudelteig

Now the fun begins!

Melt one stick of unsalted butter and keep on hand to work dough.

If you have a large table or strudel board, do this with the whole roll of dough. If your kitchen is small, just clear off about 2' of counter space and do the dough in two halves. Lay out a clean, unscented, cotton cloth that is a little larger than your working surface. Flour lightly.

Flatten the dough out with your hand. Flour your hands, and rolling pin. Roll out the dough into a 12" x 12" square. Then brush or dab the top with melted butter. This helps it stretch. You may also want to dab your fingers with butter, too, so the dough doesn't stick to them.

Now you can begin stretching the dough – either with your hands underneath, palms down, teasing it out from the center. Or by placing a light weight, such as a 1 pint bottle on one end and carefully pulling the opposite end. Continue, working your way around the dough. Even if you are working on a kitchen counter, you can do it this way, with just one person. About half way through, brush or dab the top again with butter to make it stretch easily. Don't worry about holes appearing. Just leave the hole alone. You are going to roll up the whole thing, so holes won't show.

When the dough is stretched out, so it covers your whole surface and you can read a newspaper through it, it's ready. Trust me, it's not as hard as it seems, and you can read a paper through it sooner than you'd think, so try it.

Assembling the Strudel

When you scatter your filling over the dough, make sure you leave ample room around top, bottom and side edges for sealing the dough. Strew the bread crumbs over the dough. Then the apple mixture. Then the nuts. Finally, a small box or two of raisins – 1 ½ to 3 oz. And one last thing, sprinkle about 1/8 cup melted butter over the things you have scattered on the dough.

Taking up the edge of the cloth, gently shake the cloth, until the dough starts rolling itself up. Keep going until the dough is almost rolled up completely. Moisten the final edge with water. Then roll up completely. Press the moistened edge into the roll, gently. Tuck the ends under.

Cut the long roll into two halves. Form them into two horseshoe-sized loaves for baking. This is why it doesn't matter if you prepare the dough in halves. Transfer, using the cloth, onto a greased baking sheet or iron skillet. You can place the seam either on the top or bottom. Dab or brush the top with melted butter. Put in a 350 degree oven and bake for 35 to 45 minutes, until golden brown. After 10 minutes of baking, dab again with butter. Do this again at 20 minutes. This helps give you a flaky crust.

When the Strudel is done, sprinkle the top with powdered sugar. Serve with whipped cream. And coffee the Viennese way or Kaffee fur Kind.

Quickie Strudel

From my friend, Tea

My Serb friend Tea made this with sour cherries from the farmer's market, when I was visiting her in Chicago. Her method doesn't require all the cooking artistry of Strudelteig. And it gives you flaky Cherry Strudel or Apfelstrudel in under an hour, including cooking time!

Phyllo/filo dough

Uncooked sour cherries or apple slices, or apricots or sweet cherries or blueberries or pie filling

Sugar

Toasted bread crumbs

Melted butter

Cinnamon

Optional raisins and chopped nuts

Buy phyllo/filo dough at the store. Peel off a layer and brush or dab both sides with melted butter. On one end, place uncooked sour cherries or raw sliced apples. Sprinkle with a tsp. of sugar, a little cinnamon and some toasted bread crumbs. Optional: scatter a few raisins and chopped nuts.

Continue until you have 3 or 4 layers, covering each layer with the next. Then roll up the strudel. You can seal the dough around the edges. Or like Tea, you can pop the rolls in the oven and just let them ooze out during baking. Bake at 400 degrees until golden brown.

The Gridley Dairy

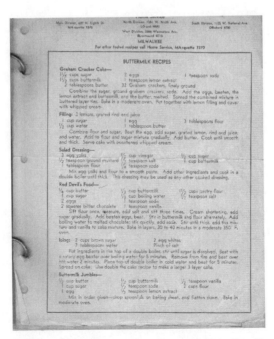

Gridley Dairy's cookbook with the Red Devil's Food recipe

Red Devil's Food Cake

Fanni made this cake a lot when she came to America. The recipe came from the Gridley Dairy Co. of Milwaukee, Home Service Department cookbook. I found this recipe copied out several times over – it was REALLY GOOD, according to Mom.

1 cup sugar

¼ cup butter [or cold-pressed oil. Fanni used shortening]

2 eggs, beaten

2 squares melted bitter chocolate

½ cup sour milk or buttermilk

½ cup boiling water

1 ½ cups pastry flour

1 tsp baking soda

½ tsp salt

1 tsp vanilla

Sift flour once, measure, add salt and sift three times. Cream butter, add sugar gradually. Add eggs and beat. Stir in buttermilk and flour alternately. Beat after each addition, until smooth. Add boiling water to melted chocolate. Stir quickly, add soda. Stir until thick. Add the chocolate mixture and the vanilla to cake mixture. Beat until smooth.

Pour into 2 round greased pans and bake at 350 degrees for 30 minutes.

Gridley Dairy Cooked White Icing

From the Gridley Dairy Co. Cookbook

2 cups brown sugar

7 T water

2 egg whites

pinch of salt

Put ingredients in the top of a double boiler, stir until sugar is dissolved. Beat with a rotary egg beater over boiling water for 5 minutes. Remove from fire and beat for 5 minutes. Spread on cake.

Margaret, called "Gretel"

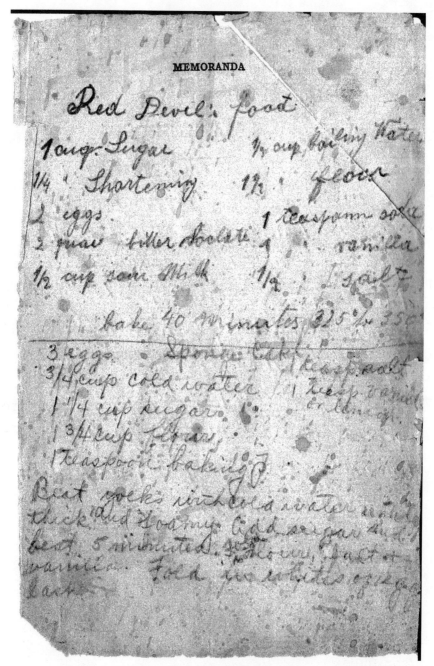

MEMORANDA

Red Devil's food

1 cup Sugar   ¾ cup boiling Water
¼ " Shortening   1½ " flour
2 eggs   1 teaspoon soda
2 sqr. bitter chocolate   ½ " vanilla
½ cup sour Milk   ½ " salt

bake 40 minutes 325° to 350°

3 eggs   Sponge Cake
¾ cup cold water   1 teaspoon salt
1¼ cup sugar   1 teasp. vanilla
1¾ cup flour
1 teaspoon baking p.

Beat yolks with cold water until thick and foamy add sugar then beat 5 minutes. add flour, salt + vanilla. Fold in whites of eggs last.

Fanni's copy of Gridley's Red Devil's Food recipe
written on a scrap of paper with Mom's handwriting, too

My Chocolate Cake

Personally, I like a dense chocolate cake with lots of chocolate frosting on it. Here is my dynamite chocolate cake, with mocha frosting, that always gets rave reviews – until I tell people how I make it, so be sure to keep that a secret!

Take 1 box of Roundy's Brownie Mix. I'm not kidding! I learned about how great this tastes when my friend Kate, whose house I once lived in, was baking for the neighbors at Christmas. Usually, I abhor the idea of making stuff from a mix, so I just try not to read the ingredients on the box when I make this.

Follow directions on the box. Pour the brownies into two greased 8″ cake pans. Bake according to directions on the box.

Mocha Frosting

2 squares of melted chocolate

1 cup confectioner's sugar

1 or 2 sticks of butter, creamed

½ tsp vanilla

3 T super strong black coffee

Mix the melted chocolate with the butter. Then gradually beat in the sugar, coffee and vanilla until smooth.

Decorate Your Cake

And while you are doing that, you can think of how you'd like to decorate your cake. It has to out-Martha-Stewart Martha Stewart. Once I did this on my birthday and brought it in to the fencing club, with my Xena doll perched on top. [a gift from my younger brother, Brian] Xena stood, with her sword in hand, mounted on the top of the cake, slaying a circle of a little gingerbread cookie men. Boy did they ever love that cake!

Another time, I made the cake for Mom's 75th birthday party, which we had out at my house on Mirror Lake. I cut out a hole in the center of the cake, and stuck in a vase of wild flowers that grew around my house, out in the wilderness.

Fanni on her 75th birthday

Sachertorte

We never had anything this chocolatey at Fanni's. The chocolatiest thing we had were Hershey Bars or chocolate Bismarks, both of which were darned good!

You may have already eaten Sachertorte, a rich, Viennese chocolate cake, with chocolate icing and an apricot filling. It debuted in 1832 when Franz Sacher, employed by an Austro-Hungarian prince, was pinch hitting for a dinner of notables. He was only a 16 year old apprentice chef, who was cooking that day in 1832, because the regular chef had taken ill. Thus Sachertorte was born.

Franz's son, Eduard Sacher founded the Sacher Hotel in 1876, where he served the chocolatey torte in the restaurant.

The recipe has been a closely guarded secret for over a century. But, you can find one claiming to be the "the original recipe, obtained through the courtesy of Mrs. Anna Sacher" at the link below. It was published in a 1952 book on Viennese cooking by O. & A. Hess, who collected it from Eduard's widow, Mrs. Anna Sacher, who survived to 1930.

http://en.wikipedia.org/wiki/Sachertorte

Rumbombe

Rumbombe is an awesome recipe. What's not to like, with chocolate, butter, apricots, rum and eleven eggs? The upper part of the cake looks like a mosaic. That's because the cake looks like a bomb on the outside and on the inside.

I found this curious recipe in someone's handwriting, photocopied onto a half sheet of paper. On the back were scribbled notes by Mom on Liver Dumpling Soup and Kaiserschmarren, which she gave me for this book. Mom doesn't know where the *Rumbombe* recipe came from. Grandma never made it.

Maybe the photocopy was on a piece of recycled paper from the Austrian Club that Mom belongs to. That's a social group that participates in Austrian culture by celebrating St. Nicholas Day [complete with Krampus and the Devil], and Austrian-American Day. They have a summer picnic with specially-raised, spit-roasted chickens. They also listen to live Austrian music and dance to it, too. And once a year, they make and sell Austrian Spaetzl and Wienerschnitzel at Germanfest.

Today Milwaukee is known as the City of Festivals, where you can go to a huge ethnic festival on the lakefront, nearly every weekend in the summer. That includes Germanfest, Irish Fest [the largest Celtic culture celebration in the world], African World Festival, Festa Mexicana, Festa Italiana, Polish Fest, Indian Summer, and so on. There are still more than 30 German and Austrian social clubs preserving cultural customs in Milwaukee.

Rumbombe Recipe

Cake - Biskuitteig

8 Eggs separated

1 ½ cups Sugar

2 cups Flour

Cream the egg yolks with the sugar. Beat the egg whites until stiff. Finally, stir in the flour gently. Turn batter into a greased 10 inch spring form pan and bake 35-45 minutes in the middle rack of the oven at 350 degrees F, until the cake is a golden brown and a toothpick inserted comes out clean.

Remove and cool. When cool, slice the cake lengthwise about 2/3 of the way down. Then take the upper 2/3 and cut that top part into cubes.

Crème

3 Eggs

1 cup and 2 T Sugar

1 cup Milk

3 sticks Butter

3 or 4 T Rum

1 cup Apricot Marmalade

Combine beaten eggs with sugar, and 1 stick of room temperature butter, and 1 cup of milk. Heat slowly, stirring often. Bring to a boil for one minute. Let cool. Cream the rest of the butter until fluffy. Add rum slowly and beat until smooth. Add the butter and rum mixture to the rest of the cream when it has cooled. [Note that the rum becomes part of the cake with its alcohol intact.]

Put the cubes of cake into a bowl and pour the cream over them, tossing to coat them evenly. Let them sit for a little while to soak up the liquid.

Remove the bottom layer of the cake on a plate. Spread a thick layer of apricot marmalade over the cake.

When the cake cubes have absorbed the liquid, pile them on top of the marmalade layer. Shape into a dome with your hands. [The top of the cake may or may not be lumpy, depending on how soggy your cubes are. It's easier to frost a smooth cake. The cake has a homely appearance when done. Don't let that fool you! It's really, really good!]

Frosting

6 – 8 oz. Milk Chocolate [or bittersweet chocolate, according to your taste]

1/3 cup Butter

Melt the chocolate in a double boiler with butter and mix. Drizzle the chocolate icing over the entire outside of the cake with a tablespoon. You can even it out with your fingers or a knife. It will be a homely, lumpy looking cake, until you cut it open. This cake will cut better after it has been refrigerated or frozen. Yes, it has so much fat in it, it cuts well frozen!

Rumbombe with blackberries on top of the chocolate

Strawberry Cake

From Renate in Vienna

Renate, who is Fanni's great niece, made us this beautiful dessert when we visited her in Vienna. Let me tell you, it is a sight to behold!

Biskuitteig

4 eggs, separated

¾ cup sugar

a cup of SIFTED flour

Whip yolks with sugar until creamy. Whip egg whites until stiff. Fold whipped egg whites into sugar and yolk mixture by hand. Gradually add flour. There is no leavening in this cake, just the whipped egg whites to make it light, so don't over stir.

Turn into a greased 9″ round cake pan. Bake at 350 degrees for 25-30 minutes, until done.

Here are three tests for doneness:
1. When the cake top is golden brown
2. When the cake springs back when tapped lightly with a finger
3. When a toothpick or knife inserted into the center comes out clean.

Strawberry Cake — lots of work, but spectacular results!

Fruit Glaze - or Just Use Strawberry Jelly

½ cup sugar

½ cup fruit juice

1 T cornstarch

½ package gelatin

Make a paste with cornstarch and a few spoonfuls of the fruit juice and set aside. Mix sugar and the rest of the fruit juice in a pan. Bring to a boil. Sprinkle gelatin over the mixture and stir. Add a little of this mixture to the cornstarch paste until creamy. Add the cornstarch to the mixture in the pan gradually. Bring to a boil again. Cool.

Dip the strawberries ahead of time into the fruit glaze and place on a dinner plate until you are ready to use them. The glaze is necessary so that the strawberries look fresh and luscious. Alternatively, you could use Strawberry Jelly, thinned with a little bit of water.

Topping

This topping best if made right before you are going to eat it.

Sweetened whipped cream [recipe under Jello].

Topfen or Topfen substitute [see next page]

Mix Topfen with sweetened whipped cream. Pile that on top of the baked biscuitteig. Scatter the strawberries on top of the cream, or place in a circle or heart.

A Word on Topfen

*Topfen in English is "quark," a cheese made by adding a bacteria culture to milk and draining off the whey. Topfen has a rich, tangy taste because it comes from cultured milk. You might be able to find Topfen at a gourmet or German specialty store. Fanni sold it in her store, in Vienna.

One alternative to quark is mascarpone, which has a high fat content because it's made with cream. Another alternative is ricotta cheese, made with rennet instead of friendly bacteria, thus giving it a stronger taste.

Topfen Recipe

Buttermilk, usually made with 2% milk in the U.S.

Give this a shot if you want to try your hand at making quark. It's very easy to do. Turn your oven on to 150 degrees. Pour buttermilk into an ovenproof bowl and cover. Place in the oven overnight, about 8 or 12 hours. If your oven doesn't go that low, just set it at the lowest temperature and turn off for the night. You should have clotted buttermilk in the morning.

Line a colander or sieve with cheesecloth. Or use just the sieve, if it has an extra tight mesh. Pour in the clotted buttermilk. Allow the whey to drain 30 minutes to an hour, stirring with a spoon to encourage the whey to drain. You can save the whey if you like.

Streusel

From Mrs. Schuneman

According to Mom, Streusel is "something you sprinkle over a cake."

Mrs. Schueneman was a lady Grandma cleaned for, at 10 cents and hour. This recipe was typed out on Mom's old Royal typewriter, a birthday present for her 16th birthday, which she says was "a hardship for her parents" to buy. Mom was studying secretarial skills in high school, which later stood her in good stead as an executive secretary and a legal secretary. This recipe was pasted into a 1927 Butterick cookbook, with the name, Mrs. Shuneman written out in Mom's handwriting.

¼ tsp. cinnamon

½ cup sugar

½ cup flour

¼ cup butter

Mix flour and sugar. Pour melted butter over this mixture and blend. Then you can strew it over something wonderful, like a coffee cake.

Cake Filling

Also from Mrs. Schuneman

Cakes used to have luscious fillings like this one.

2 apples [grated]

Juice of 2 lemons

1 cup sugar

No directions given. However, you should heat up the mixture, until the sugar dissolves and the grated apples soften. Cool. Then, spread between the layers of your 2 layer cake. Or cut a slit in the middle of your cake and fill with a pastry bag.

Cream Filling

For a cake with lots of layers

This was on the page opposite the Cake Filling Recipe, which my Mom typed out and pasted into the Butterick cookbook. This recipe was marked in pencil with an "x."

1 T corn starch

1 cup milk

1 egg yolk

1/8 tsp. salt

1 tsp. vanilla

2 T confectioner's sugar

½ tsp. butter

Mix the cornstarch with two tablespoons of the milk. Heat the rest of the milk in a double boiler and stir the cornstarch paste slowly into it. Stir the mixture until it is smooth and cook it for fifteen minutes. Add the beaten egg yolk and cook two minutes longer. Remove from the fire and add the salt, sugar and butter. Beat well. Add flavoring. Cool before spreading on layers of cake.

Marmorkuchen or Marble Cake

Found this recipe for a marble Guglehuf, or fluted cake,
copied out by Fanni, on a blank page

in the Rumford Cookbook

My Viennese cousin Renate's son, Bernhard, [Fanni's great, great nephew] made this for us in Vienna, when we visited him at his house. At the time, Bernhard and his wife Elke lived in a condo in a former industrial space. Mom describes their apartment as "a luxury condo, in one of five tiered, round buildings that were called *Gasometers*, which had once supplied heating gas to all of Vienna. The two lower floors of the buildings are for shopping – supermarkets, clothing stores, restaurants and entertainment venues. There is also direct access to the subway."

¾ cup butter or cold-pressed oil [originally shortening]

2 cups sugar

4 egg whites

3 cups flour

3 tsp. baking powder

½ tsp. salt

1 ½ cup liquid

2 tsp. vanilla

1 square chocolate melted

¼ tsp. soda

Marmorkuchen or Marble Cake con't

Cream the butter, add sugar gradually and cream well. Add the unbeaten egg white, one at a time, into mixture. Sift flour once before measuring. Mix and sift the flour, baking powder and salt together and add alternately with liquid. Add the vanilla. Add soda to the melted chocolate. Divide the batter into 2 parts. Add chocolate mixture to one of the parts.

Pour plain batter into a fluted cake pan. In a swirling motion, add the chocolate mixture, but do not stir.

Put pan into a preheated 350 degree oven for 40 minutes or until cake is done. The cake is served unfrosted.

MEMORANDA

Marble Cake.

3/4 cup Shortening
2 " Sugar
4 egg whites
3 cups Flour

3 tsp baking powder
1/2 tsp Salt
1 1/2 cup liquid
2 tsp. Vanilla
1 sp. Chocolate melted

1/4 tsp soda

Cream the shortening, add sugar gradually + cream well. Add the unbeaten egg white on at a time into mixture. Sift Flour once before measuring. Mix + sift the Flour baking powder + salt together + add alternately with liquid. Add the vanilla. Add soda to the melted Chocolate Divide the batter into 2 parts. adding Chocolate mixture to one of the part Drope the batter by 1 teaspoonful into a floured + greased pan. Heat 350

Fanni's Marble Cake recipe

Pfefferneuse

This is another item Grandma always bought at the bakery. The recipe is from Aunt Margie, typed and pasted into a Rumford cookbook

2 cups sugar

4 cups flour

4 big eggs or 5 small eggs

1 tsp. cinnamon

1 lemon peel, grated

2 tsp. baking powder

1 tsp. cloves

powdered sugar

Combine dry ingredients. Beat eggs and add dry ingredients to them, until you have a dough you can roll out with your hands like a big, fat lead pencil. Cut into 1 inch pieces and place on cut side on greased cookie sheets. Bake at 350 degrees, for 15 to 20 minutes, until cookies are lightly browned.

Roll in powdered sugar while still warm and store in cookie tins. We always got these little dome shaped cookies in a crinkly cellophane bag. The cookies were quite hard. Just right for dunking in milk or coffee.

Peanut or Almond Ice Box Cookies

Fanni made these with hazelnuts or almonds. I found this recipe typed out by my Mom on her Royal typewriter and pasted into the Rumford Cookbook

1 lb. butter

1T cinnamon

2 tsp. soda

1 cup sugar

1 cup brown sugar

3 eggs well beaten

5 cups flour

¼ lb hazelnuts or almonds, or 1 lb. peanuts, shelled

Cream butter and sugar together. Add eggs, 1 lb. shelled, roasted peanuts or ¼ lb. almonds or hazelnuts, sliced fine, crosswise. Mix together flour, soda and cinnamon and add to mixture. Roll dough out into a 2 inch-thick roll. Place in an icebox until firm. Cut in thin medallion slices. Bake in 350F oven until crisp.

Chocolate Pinwheels

This cookie recipe was also typed out by Mom on her Royal typewriter.

1 ½ c sifted flour

½ tsp. double-acting baking powder

1/8 tsp. salt

½ cup butter

½ cup sugar

1 egg yolk, unbeaten

4 T milk

1 square unsweetened choc., melted

Sift flour once, measure, add baking powder and salt, and sift again. Cream butter thoroughly, add sugar gradually and cream together until light and fluffy. Add egg yolk and beat well. Add flour alternately with milk, mixing well after each addition.

Divide dough in two parts. To one part add chocolate and blend. Chill until firm enough to roll. Roll each half into a rectangular sheet 1/8 inch thick, and place chocolate sheet on top. Then roll as for jelly roll. Chill overnight or until firm enough to slice. Cut in 1/8 inch slices. Bake on ungreased baking sheet in hot oven, 400 degrees for 5 minutes, or until done. Makes 3 ½ doz. wheels.

My Chocolate Pudding

In America, Fanni used to just make cooked pudding from a box, according to directions written right on the box. It was one of her inexpensive Depression desserts. Here is my adaptation of cocoa I had in Spello, Italy, that nearly makes a spoon stand up!

1 cup milk

1 heaping tsp. cocoa

1 tsp. sweetener – I prefer honey or maple syrup

2 tsp. flour

Start by making a paste of flour and cocoa, with a little milk. Slowly add the rest of the milk to it, plus your sweetener. Heat, stirring frequently, over a low flame until it thickens.

Fanni's Jello

Another Depression dessert that Fanni was still making in the 50's, when I came along. She made it according to directions on the box. I've looked on the box, and gelatin really does have some protein value!

Fanni served her jello with whipped cream.

Whipped Cream

1 cup whipping cream

¼ cup powdered sugar

1 tsp. vanilla [optional]

Beat whipping cream until it stands in peaks. You can do this with an egg beater, the way I did it in Fanni's kitchen. Or you can buzz it up in a blender, or food processor, or even with an electric mixer.

With the final few strokes, beat powdered sugar into the whipped cream. Add vanilla, if desired. We had it on Jello. The grownups used this in their coffee during dessert, too.

My Jello

I like to make plain gelatin, following the directions on the box, and use canned juice instead of water. Then I cut up a couple of bananas or throw in a couple of peeled, sectioned oranges or cut up some pears or other fruit I have on hand.

Fanni's Fruit Salad

Codified by Mom

Peel and slice apples, oranges and bananas, or whatever fruit you have on hand. Add a little lemon juice, toss and chill. For dressing, thin mayonnaise with a little orange juice.

Genevieve's Variation

Peel and slice oranges, grapefruits, bananas and kiwi. Add green grapes. Dress with strawberry yogurt.

Fresh Fruit Delight

Codified by Mom

Spread ¼ cup coconut in a shallow pan and bake at 250 degrees for 15 min., stirring often. Use the coconut as a topping for a combination of fresh strawberries, blueberries, green grapes, sliced peaches, cantaloupe balls, watermelon balls, bananas, etc.

Glazed Apple Rings

Codified by Mom

Combine

2 cups of honey

1 cup of vinegar

1 tsp. cinnamon

¼ tsp. nutmeg

½ tsp salt

Cook and stir over low heat until well blended. Slice 6 to 8 cored, unpeeled apples into ½ inch rings and drop a few at a time into the syrup, cooking until they are transparent and glazed, but have not lost their shape. Place rings on serving dish and pour remaining syrup over. Makes 6 to 8 servings.

This seems to me like it's a country recipe, because it uses honey as a sweetener. Honey was something you could find in the woods. But sugar had to be purchased with money.

Stewed Fruit

Reconstructed by Mom

Simmer pears, apricots, prunes or peaches in enough water to cover the fruit, adding sugar to taste, until they are done the way you like them.

My variation is to add cinnamon or ginger or rose water to the boiling water and substitute honey or just skip the sweetener all together.

Fanni in the backyard on 16th Street

Plum Dumplings

I saved the best dish until last!

In the fall came my favorite meal Fanni made: plum dumplings. It was a dish we got only once a year in September, because that's when Italian prune plums ripen. When Mom would announce that we were having it for dinner that Sunday we could hardly wait to in the car and drive down to Grandma's.

Plum dumplings were really marvelous, big fat dumplings, coated with buttered breadcrumbs. We'd sink a fork into the dumpling, and purple plum juice would run out of it. Slicing the dumpling open revealed white potato dough stained pink by the hot, sweet and tart Italian prune plum, resting inside it like a jewel. Over the split dumpling, we tapped cinnamon out of a red and white metal spice, can that rang with a hollow sound. Then we dipped the silver plated spoon into the china sugar bowl, with a crunch of granules, and sprinkled sugar over the cinnamon. Or vice versa, depending on which container got passed around the table to you first. Fanni's china bowl was decorated with blue and white peonies and exotics birds. It never had a lid because it was a pass-on gift from a lady Fanni had once cleaned house for. The spoon didn't match anything either.

Plum Dumplings was a meal she served without side dishes or dessert, because none were needed. Plum Dumplings are a meal and dessert, all in one dish! Afterward, everyone lined up the pits on their plate to see who had eaten the most dumplings, the highest number, being around 9 or 10. Even when I was a little girl, sometimes I had eaten the most!

No one was ever able to take the recipe down quite right. My Mom and her sister made other dishes of Fanni's invention, but for some reason they never got this one right. A number of times I took down the recipe for Plum Dumplings from Grandma, because I wanted to know how to make it some day. She estimated the amount of ingredients when she told it to me. My Aunt Margie wrote it down once, too. But neither she nor her daughter Betty could make the recipe work. The dumplings just fell apart.

Basically the recipes were all missing most of the flour that should go in them, so a person would end up with a soggy potato dough, which would slough off as soon as it hit the boiling water. Finally, I tried making them. And since I cook by feel, I just kept adding more and more cups of flour until I had a dough of the right consistency to work with. So if you find your dough too flabby, add more flour. If it's too stiff, add a little more milk. And above all, boil a test dumpling first! That's how I figured it out.

Plum Dumplings were a magical dish that no one else outside our family had ever heard of. It was our private pleasure to enjoy once a year.

Recipe for Plum Dumplings

I took this down from Grandma in the late 60's or early 70's. Fanni guessed she used 1 cup of flour, but in reality, it's more like 4 cups of flour.

Makes 2 dozen or more.

2 dozen fresh Italian prune plums

> These plums are available in the fall. You can also use plums off your tree. Alternatively, you can use canned plums. Also good are cherries, berries or apricots, fresh, canned or frozen. Just make sure you dry the fruits if they are not fresh, so the moisture doesn't make the dough impossible to work with. Put enough pieces of the fruit in the middle, so it's about the size of an Italian prune plum.

6 medium [2 to 3 lbs] white Wisconsin potatoes, boiled

> You can also use russets grown anywhere. If you use red potatoes, you will have a wetter potato mixture to begin with

2 eggs, slightly beaten

1 – 1 ½ tsp salt

4 cups of flour, more or less

4 T butter

2 cups breadcrumbs - best if homemade from Kaiser rolls or if you can't find real Kaiser rolls from a bakery, use a real French baguette.

1. Wash, peel and boil potatoes.

2. In the meantime, melt a half stick of butter in a frying pan, add bread crumbs and toast until brown. You have to watch the bread crumbs as they brown, and stir them, because otherwise they will burn.

3. Cool potatoes. Drain really well. Grandma put them through a ricer, which gives you a nice, uniform mashed potato. Alternatively, you can peel the potatoes and put them into a food processor and buzz. The drier your potatoes are, the easier it's going to be to make a dough with them.

4. In a large bowl, add beaten eggs and salt. Gradually add unsifted flour until you have a sticky dough you can knead. That could take more or less than 4 cups, depending on the kind of potatoes, how well they were drained and the whimsy of the plum dumpling goddess. Flour your hands. Take the dough out of the bowl at this point and place on a heavily floured board. Continue kneading, working in more and more flour, until the dough no longer sticks to your hands. As far as dough consistency goes, it should be firm, but not as stiff as bread dough. The best thing to do is to make a trial dumpling and cook it. If it falls apart, you know to add more flour.

5. Keeping your hands and the bread board floured, shape the dough into one long roll, about the width of a rolling pin, and cut into pieces about 2" in length with a table knife.

6. Flatten out each 2" piece and lightly dust the back side with flour. Then press a plum into the piece of dough. Pinch the dough together, until the plum is completely covered. Then take the ball in your hands and roll until it is nice and round. Then dust the ball with flour and set aside until you have enough to cook up a batch.

7. Cook the dumplings in boiling salted water for about 10 minutes until they rise to the top. Every few minutes, carefully lift each dumpling from the bottom of the pan, so it doesn't stick. Watch out when you drain them that they don't fall apart! You can drain individually, by rolling on a clean flour sac towel.

8. After you drain each dumpling for just a few minutes, roll it in the bread crumbs, while the dumplings are still soft on the outside. That way, the crumbs will stick to the outside of the dumpling.

Keep the dumplings warm in the oven at about 150 degrees, lightly covered on a plate until they are all ready to serve. Serve with cinnamon and granulated sugar at the table, in separate containers. Count the pits and see how many you ate!

Fanni and my Mom took a folk dancing a class at the Siefert Recreation Center on 4th and Cherry. It was a mother-daughter class, where they learned how to do Austrian dances, like the Lendler. When they performed, they wore traditional outfits, which Margaret sewed. I wore the bodice to one of them to historical reenactments, because it was so comfortable. It was a favorite of mine to wear in hot weather.

Brandtieg – for Plum Dumplings

from Tante Rudi in Vienna

You can also make Plum Dumplings with Brandteig. "Brannt Teich" is how I copied it out in my notes.

1 Seitel = 1/3 liter milk = 10.5 ounces

½ Stick butter

Rampferl = a pinch of salt

2 Seitel = 2/3 liter flour

1 egg

12 Italian plums

Bread crumbs browned in butter

Heat milk, butter, salt to boil.   Add flour while boiling, but remove it at once from heat. Add egg and stir briskly. Turn and knead for a few minutes until the dough sticks together. Make into a long sausage and cut into 12 pieces. Form the dough around each plum. Boil for 10 minutes or until the dumplings rise to the surface. Drain dumplings on a towel. Brown the crumbs in butter. Roll the dumplings one by one in crumbs. Serve sprinkled with cinnamon and sugar.

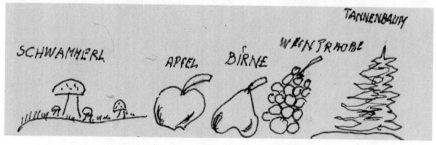

Tante Rudi's German lesson for me

About the Author

Genevieve Davis is the granddaughter of Fanni Baier. She ate her way through her childhood days spent over at Fanni's, soaking up the simple pleasures of Austrian culture and basking in the sunshine of the world Fanni created.

Davis has more works for you to enjoy. You can read *Secret Life, Secret Death,* a true story that unravels the mystery of what happened to her *other* grandmother in Gangland Chicago's Roaring 20's.

Davis also directed the award winning film SECRET LIFE, SECRET DEATH, which has played across the U.S. and in Europe. Book and DVD available at **www.secretlifesecretdeath.com**

Davis is also a painter. See her paintings, at **www.october7thstudio.com**

Stay in Touch

Get Books and DVD
http://october7thstudio.com/Estore.htm

Email **info@october7thstudio.com**

Twitter **@GenevieveDavis3**

Facebook **Genevieve Davis**

Blog **http://genevieve-davis.blogspot.com/**

Film clips **www.secretlifesecretdeath.com**

Website **www.october7thstudio.com**

Made in the USA
San Bernardino, CA
18 March 2014